PROPHECY IN ISLAM

Philosophy and Orthodoxy

PROPHECY IN ISLAM
Philosophy and Orthodoxy

FAZLUR RAHMAN

With a New Foreword by Michael Sells

THE UNIVERSITY OF CHICAGO PRESS

CHICAGO AND LONDON

TO

Simon Van Den Bergh

The University of Chicago Press, Chicago 60637
The University of Chicago Press, Ltd., London
© 1958 by George Allen & Unwin Ltd.
Foreword © 2011 by The University of Chicago
All rights reserved.
Paperback edition 2011
Printed in the United States of America

20 19 18 17 16 15 14 13 12 11   1 2 3 4 5

ISBN-13: 978-0-226-70282-7 (cloth)
ISBN-10: 0-226-70282-0 (cloth)
ISBN-13: 978-0-226-70285-8 (paper)
ISBN-10: 0-226-70285-5 (paper)

LIBRARY OF CONGRESS CATALOGING-IN-PUBLICATION DATA

Rahman, Fazlur, 1919–1988.
Prophecy in Islam : philosophy and orthodoxy / Fazlur Rahman ; with a new foreword by Michael Sells.
p. cm.
Includes index.
ISBN-13: 978-0-226-70285-8 (pbk. : alk. paper)
ISBN-10: 0-226-70285-5 (pbk. : alk. paper) 1. Islamic philosophy.
2. Prophecy—Islam. 3. Revelation—Islam. 4. Intellect—Philosophy. I. Sells, Michael Anthony. II. Title.
B745.P66R34 2011
297.2'115—dc22
2011011929

♾ This paper meets the requirements of
ANSI/NISO Z39.48-1992 (Permanence of Paper).

CONTENTS

FOREWORD

By Michael Sells

Prophecy in Islam was the second of three books published by Fazlur Rahman on the analysis of the soul, intellect, and revelation in al-Fārābī (d. ca. 950) and Ibn Sīnā (d. 1037; or Avicenna, as he came to be known in Latin).

In 1952, Rahman published *Avicenna's Psychology*, an annotated translation of the psychological section of Ibn Sīnā's *Kitāb al-Najāt* (Book of Deliverance). *Prophecy in Islam* followed in 1958. The next year saw the appearance of Avicenna's *De Anima* (On the Soul), a critical edition of the psychological section of Ibn Sīnā's vast work, *Kitāb al-Shifā'* (The Book of Healing or Cure). In these three works, Rahman edited, contextualized, compared, and analyzed core passages from the two philosophers regarding the development of analytical and abstract reasoning within human beings and the relationship of the intellect to the interior senses, including various activities associated with the imagination and memory. Those passages exercised a pervasive influence on the development of philosophy of the mind within classical Islamic, Jewish, and Christian thought.[1] They also raise enduring questions concerning the relationship of scientific knowledge to inspiration (or revelation), the tensions and collaborations between analytical intellect and the imagination, the relationship between philosophical inquiry and prophetic teachings, and possible philosophical perspectives on the nature of revelation.

Philosophy and psychology carry specific meanings in these three works by Rahman. By philosophy, he meant the philosophical tradition, composed in Arabic by authors of various ethnic, linguistic, and religious backgrounds, that was known as *falsafa*, an Arabic term directly transliterated from the Greek, or as *ḥikma* (thought or wisdom). One feature distinguishing the *falsafa* tradition from other writings in Arabic that could be considered philosophical in the broader sense was the marked influence of Aristotle. *Falsafa* emerged in conjunction with the great translation movement among Arabic-speaking Muslim and Christian scholars that brought virtually all of the available Greek texts of Aristotle and of his commentators into Arabic. Rahman points out the particular importance not only of Aristotle's work *De Anima* (On the Mind or Soul) in this regard but also the Arabic version of the *De Anima* of the Aristotelian commentator Alexander of Aphrodisias, who flourished around the year 200 CE. The Aristotelian heritage was further complicated by the translation into Arabic of the writings on the soul and the intellect by Plotinus, the third-century Alexandrian who founded Neoplatonism, but which were attributed not to Plotinus but to Aristotle, and were known in Arabic as the *Theology of Aristotle.*[2]

"Psychology" in Fazlur Rahman's writings—as the term appears, for example, in the title of his 1952 book *Avicenna's Psychology*—refers to the philosophical understanding of the animal and the human vital principle: *psyche* in Greek, and *nafs* in Arabic. In translations of Arabic philosophical writings, the *nafs* is usually translated as "soul," but it can also carry connotations of "self," "spirit," or "person." Included in the science of the *nafs* were investigations into the sense faculties of animals and humans, how they form and store the impressions of sense objects, how they recall such impressions even when the original sense objects are no longer present, how they create new images or concepts from them, and how they evaluate the import or significance of those images or concepts.

As suggested in *Prophecy in Islam*'s subtitle, "Philosophy and Orthodoxy," the Islamic nature of al-Fārābī and Ibn Sīnā's work and its compatibility with Islamic "right belief" has generated controversy. Many Arabic philosophers—such as al-Kindī, al-Fārābī, Ibn Sīnā, and Ibn Rushd (Averroës)—were of course Muslims, and viewed their teachings as completely in harmony with Islam, and Ibn Sīnā had received training in the Hanafi school of Islamic jurisprudence. The question remains regarding the extent to which al-Fārābī and Ibn Sīnā in particular were engaged in a form of philosophical reflection that was distinctively Islamic. The discourse of the philosophers tended to cross religious boundaries freely, with Jewish, Christian, and Muslim writers citing one another as authorities or at least treating one another's ideas with serious intellectual respect. To what extent is philosophical reflection, in general, compatible with prophetically revealed religion? If, as the philosophers suggested, reason can rise to ever higher truths to eventually attain the very highest understanding—and without the aid of revealed scriptures and the symbols and laws that are communicated in revelation—are not the philosophers situating themselves and their science outside the bounds of revealed religion? On the other hand, as Rahman shows in *Prophecy in Islam,* al-Fārābī and Ibn Sīnā viewed philosophical knowledge as dependent upon a supernal intellect known as the active intellect or active intelligence, associated with the lowest and most accessible of the heavenly spheres. Ibn Sīnā explicitly identified the active intellect with Jibril (Gabriel), the spirit who brings the divine revelation to the prophet, according to Islamic tradition; and both writers viewed prophets as philosophers endowed with the special ability to translate the abstract truths of the active intelligence into a symbol-laden or figurative discourse capable of providing guidance for all human beings, not just those with aptitude and training in abstract reasoning.

Prophecy in Islam presents some challenges to those not accustomed to the technical vocabulary developed in the Arabic philosophy of the mind, or to the various Greek, Latin, Arabic, and English terms that are used by Rahman, and by other modern scholars, and avoids the confusion that can be generated by the nontechnical meanings of words like "common sense," "imagination," and "memory." Thus the faculty known in Latin as *sensus communis*, and in Arabic as *fantasia* (which was taken over from the Greek), refers neither to the level-headed, no-nonsense understanding of the obvious, denoted in modern usage by the expression "common sense," nor to the vain or unrealistic imaginings evoked by the contemporary English word "fantasy." Similar confusions between the technical uses of terminology and broader usage can be found in Arabic expressions. In addition to employing expressions from all four languages to prevent such semantic drift, *Prophecy in Islam* also builds upon and in some ways assumes prior knowledge of points elaborated in the two preceding volumes. In what follows, I offer a brief guide to some of the key concepts and terms within *Prophecy in Islam*, along with excerpts of those passages from Rahman's preceding work, *Avicenna's Psychology*, that are of special importance in this regard. My goal is not to paraphrase, restate, or evaluate Rahman's positions on al-Fārābī and Ibn Sīnā's philosophy of mind and revelation, but to offer some support for readers in engaging Rahman's work directly.[3]

The opening chapter of *Prophecy in Islam* examines al-Fārābī and Ibn Sīnā's respective positions on the development of intellect (*noūs* in Greek, *'aql* in Arabic, also translated by various authors as intelligence, reason, or mind).[4] Those human beings who are free from physical or intellectual impediments are able to advance through the various stages of intellectual development until their individual intellects reach full actualization and come into contact or proximity with the active intelligence. In the process of that development, a person's intellect moves from the purely latent or potential (*al-'aql bi al-quwwa*) to a first actualization, and then advances through higher phases of actualization. Of this process in Ibn Sīnā, Rahman writes (14–15):

According to Avicenna, the potential intellect, although it comes into existence (and is, therefore, generated) as something personal to each individual, is, nevertheless, an immaterial and immortal substance. Its actualization begins when man conceives the primary truths that are the basis for all demonstration . . . e.g., that the whole is greater than its part or that two things equal to the same thing are equal to each other, truths, that is, which we do not acquire either by induction or deduction. This stage is called *'aql bi'l malaka* (*intellect. in habitu*). When by means of these primary truths we acquire also the secondary ones and when, on the whole, our mind can operate by itself without any more help from sensitive and imaginative faculties, we reach the stage of development called by Avicenna the "actual intellect" (*intellect. in actu*).

The next phase, Rahman continues, occurs "when we do actually operate with this newly acquired power, at which our mind becomes intellect in a state of absolute act" (*bi'l fi'l al-muṭlaq*). Ibn Sīnā also names this faculty "the acquired intellect" (*al-'aql al-mustafad*).

Once reaching this phase, the intellect can contemplate not only the forms of objects that it has rendered intelligible, but it can also contemplate its own act of contemplation.[5] At this point, the human intellect has come into contact with or proximity to the active intellect or, in translations stressing active agency, the "active intelligence" (Greek, *noūs poēticos*; Arabic, *al-'aql al-fa''āl*). In *Prophecy in Islam*, Rahman translates *al-'aql al-fa''āl* as the "Active Intelligence," using the uppercase to indicate its supernal nature as expounded by the Arabic philosophers, and "intelligence" rather than "intellect" to emphasize its activity.[6] Of the relationship between the acquired intellect and the Active Intelligence according to Ibn Sīnā, Rahman notes: "This creative power [the acquired intellect] is said to be somehow in man although it is not a part of his soul" (19).

In chapter 2 of *Prophecy in Islam*, Rahman links these theories of intellectual development to perspectives on revelation: how the revelatory act takes place, what faculty received it, and most importantly, how prophets transformed pure abstract truth into symbols and, in some cases, how they projected those symbols out as visions exterior to themselves.

In explaining the prophetic act, al-Fārābī and Ibn Sīnā developed sophisticated anatomies of the human interior senses. The internal senses take in the impressions of the five exterior senses, combine them into a unified impression, abstract them from the actual physical objects that made the imprints, and store them in the mind. They also allow a person to recall certain images from the image bank and to manipulate them, change them, and disassemble and reassemble them into forms for which no sense objects exist; to form judgments concerning the images; and to store and retrieve those judgments as needed. Below I summarize the internal senses, provide the various terms used to name them, and quote or summarize Ibn Sīnā's definitions as translated in Rahman's *Avicenna's Psychology* (30–31) and as aligned with Majid Fakhry's 1985 edition of *Kitāb al-Najāt.*

1. *Sensus communis* or "common faculty." This faculty "receives all the forms which are imprinted on the five senses and transmitted to it from them." It allows for a unified and coherent perception instead of a cacophony of data from disparate senses.

Ibn Sīnā's Arabic terms: *al-ḥiss al-mushtarak,* as well as *fantasia,* a Greek word that was Arabicized early on in the *falsafa* tradition.

2. *Representation.* The faculty of representation preserves what the *sensus communis* has received from the individual five senses even in the absence of the sensed objects. Receptivity and preservation are functions of different faculties: water, for instance, can take on various forms or shapes but it cannot preserve them.

Ibn Sīnā's Arabic terms: *al-khayāl,* or *al-quwwa al-muṣawwira.*[7]

3. *Imagination.* The faculty of "sensitive imagination" relates to the animal soul, and "rational imagination" relates to the human soul: "its function is to combine certain things with others in the faculty of representation, and to separate some things from others as it chooses."

Ibn Sīnā's Arabic terms: *al-quwwa al-mutakhayyila* in relation to animals, and *al-quwwa al-mufakkira* in relation to humans.

4. *Estimation.* The estimative faculty "perceives the nonsensible intentions (*maʿānī*) of the individual sensible objects, like the faculty which judges that the wolf is to be avoided and the child is to be loved."

Ibn Sīnā's Arabic terms: *al-wahm,* or *al-quwwa al-wahmiyya.*

5. *Retention* and *recollection.* The retentive and recollective faculty retains what the estimative faculty perceives of nonsensible intentions existing in individual sensible objects.

Ibn Sīnā's Arabic term: *al-quwwa al-ḥāfiẓa al-dhākira.*

By the midpoint of chapter 2 in *Prophecy in Islam,* Rahman has set the stage for the key question: What then, in the view of al-Fārābī and Ibn Sīnā, is prophecy? In the paraphrases and translations from al-Fārābī that Rahman presents (36–37) at this point, we are given a brilliant glimpse into the philosophy of revelation at work. Rahman begins by explaining al-Fārābī's discussion of sleep, dreaming, imagination, and the creation of figures or concepts (*taṣawwur,* "figurization"). Imagination—as a faculty that is not immaterial—must express truth in figurative language. "But imagination cannot always perform this function because in ordinary waking life it is engaged as an intermediary between the perceptual and the intellectual faculties: it receives sensual images and places them at the service of the mind for the practical needs of life. When, however, in sleep, the soul withdraws from the sensible world and no longer performs this function for the mind, it assumes its proper function freely." According to al-Fārābī, some rare humans are endowed with a "pure soul and a strong imagination." For them, this liberated ability to express truth in figurative language can occur in waking life. The most gifted of these are the prophets.

The translation from al-Fārābī by Rahman that follows at this point deserves quotation in full:

Since this entire process is interconnected, what the Active Intelligence had originally given to this man (in terms of intelligibles) thus comes to be perceptually apprehended by him. In cases where the imaginative faculty symbolizes these truths with sensible images of utmost beauty and perfection, the man who comes to see them exclaims, "Verily, God has overwhelming majesty and greatness; what I have witnessed is something wonderful not to be found in the entire range of existence.

It is not impossible that when a man's imaginative power reaches extreme perfection so that he receives in his waking life from the Active Intelligence knowledge of present and future facts or of their sensible symbols and also receives the symbols of immaterial intelligibles and of the highest immaterial existents and, indeed, sees all these—it is not impossible that he becomes a prophet giving news of the Divine realm, thanks to the intelligibles that he has received.

A question remains concerning the visions which the active intellect imparts to the imagination, after those visions pour down through the internal sense and are projected out by the common sense into the exterior world, then perceived by the prophet, impressed on his imagination, subjected to evaluation and rational scrutiny, and pronounced as a marvel. Is the vision the prophet perceived as exterior and affirms as a marvel perceptible to others? Fazlur Rahman notes in this regard that al-Fārābī did not explicitly pronounce on the public perceptibility of such prophetic visions.

For both al-Fārābī and Ibn Sīnā, the internal senses of representation and imagination function in part through the activity known as mimesis (*muḥākā*). The sense impressions from the material world are aligned with their appropriate concepts through the mimetic activity. And when the pure light of the active intellect pours into the intellect and internal senses of a prophet, the prophet's mimetic activity participates in the transformation of purely noncorporeal intelligibles into the most appropriate symbols or images. Therefore, in the prophetic reversal of perception and representation, it is through mimesis that the prophet is able to arrive at the images and symbols suitable for the immaterial and abstract truth he has received directly from the active intellect.

Rahman's translations from Ibn Sīnā (32–33) in *Prophecy in Islam* can be usefully supplemented by his earlier work, *Avicenna's Psychology*, in which he translated the entire section of the *Najāt* regarding the prophetic act. I excerpt three passages that elucidated the issues being considered here. The first two passages concern the faculty of intuition, *ḥads*, which al-Fārābī and Ibn Sīnā both viewed as vital to intellectual activity. Ibn Sīnā explained that despite its central role in the act of thinking, intuition cannot easily be pinned down within the hierarchy of the phases of intellect. It is in some sense the highest state of the material or potential intelligence, which Ibn Sīnā associates with the Divine Spirit. But it also belongs to the category of the trained intellect (*intellectus in habitu*):

> If a person can acquire knowledge from within himself, this strong capacity is called "intuition." It is so strong in certain people that they do not need great effort, or instruction or actualization, in order to make contact with the active intelligence. But the primary capacity of such a person for this is so strong that he might also be said to possess the second capacity; indeed, it seems as though he knows everything from within himself. This is the highest degree of this capacity. In this state the material intelligence must be called "Divine Spirit." It belongs to the genus of *intellectus in habitu*, but is so lofty that not all people share it. It is not unlikely, indeed, that some of these actions attributed to the "Divine Intelligence" because of their powerful and lofty nature overflow into the imagination which symbolizes them in sense-imagery and words.[8]

Ibn Sīnā explains that intuition allows a person to grasp the point of an argument or solve a problem, or as Ibn Sīnā puts it, to grasp the middle term of a syllogism. Those without intuition cannot understand a syllogism. Others need more or less instruction to arrive at the proper conclusion. Those endowed with intuition are marked by "quickness of apprehension"—the ability to deduce the middle term almost immediately—and those able to hold many arguments (and their key middle terms) in mind at the same time:

> It is possible that a man may find the truth within himself, and that the syllogism may be effected in his mind without any teacher. This varies both quantitatively and qualitatively; quantitatively, because some people possess a great number of middle terms which they have discovered themselves; and qualitatively, because some people find the term more quickly than others. Now since these differences are unlimited and always vary in degrees of intensity, and since their lowest point

must be reached in men who are wholly without intuition, so their highest point must be reached in people who possess intuition regarding all or most problems, or in people who have intuition in the shortest possible time.[9]

Ibn Sīnā finally emphasizes that the prophet does not blindly accept the forms he receives, but accepts them because they are in fact consonant with the logical principles and arguments he is able to comprehend:

> So the forms of all things contained in the active intelligence are imprinted on his soul either all at once or nearly so, not that he accepts them merely on authority but on account of their logical order which encompasses all the middle terms. For beliefs accepted on authority concerning those things which are known only through their causes possess no rational certainty. This is a kind of prophetic inspiration, indeed its highest form and the one most fitted to be called Divine Power; and it is the highest human faculty.[10]

In the latter sections of chapter 2 of *Prophecy in Islam*, Rahman explores the impact of such theories of prophecy on political thought. Prophets were philosophers who not only attained the truths held and/or emanated by the Active Intelligence, but were also able to translate them, with mimetic accuracy, into temporal and spatially related symbols, images, laws, and predictions, providing guidance for all members of their community. The third and final chapter further elaborates the controversies over *falsafa* through an exploration of the positions of five major figures in Islamic intellectual history: Ibn Hazm, Shahrastāni, al-Ghazāli, Ibn Taymiyya, and Ibn Khaldūn.

As a student in Fazlur Rahman's classes at the University of Chicago in the late 1970s, I vividly recall his unscripted minilessons on the topics covered above. It is with special pleasure that I greet this reissue of *Prophecy in Islam*, a work that embodies Rahman's groundbreaking work on the philosophy of mind and revelation in classical Islamic thought. I also recall the other major topics of Rahman's teaching and research. In the area of *falsafa*, Rahman took a strong interest in the ontology of Ibn Sīnā, as well as his philosophy of mind and revelation.[11] In the area of Qur'anic interpretation, his *Major Trends in the Qur'an*, which has recently appeared in this reprint series, emerged from years of study of and teaching the Qur'anic text. Rahman's work on Islamic modernism constituted another influential dimension of his work. And although Rahman did not devote himself to writing on the topic of Islamic mysticism, his teaching in that area had an impact, as well; a number of his former students have gone on to teach and write in the area of Sufi thought and literature.

In his courses, Rahman preferred not to mix topics. His Qur'an classes focused on reading the Qur'an closely and reading each Qur'anic passage in comparison with other similar passages in the Qur'an. Theological, philosophical, political, and mystical thought and interpretations of the Qur'an were covered in classes on Islamic theology, Islamic philosophy, Islamic political thought, and Islamic mysticism, respectively. Yet although he did not mix scholarly discourses within his topic-based seminars, several guiding concerns tied the various topics together. The psychology of prophets and, in particular, of the prophet Muhammad, was one of those themes. If a prophet was not a mere passive vehicle for revelation and if his personality, character, and actions in the world were closely aligned with the revelatory act, then the relationship of the historical personage in time and place to a divinely authored revelation that, according to most schools of Islamic thought, was eternal, was an issue fascinating in itself, and was also of vital importance for the effort of a community of believers to mold their societies in harmony with the prophetic message.

I end with some selected readings that would go well with any course that included Fazlur Rahman's *Prophecy in Islam* or *Avicenna's Psychology.*

Alexander of Aphrodisias. "Texte arabe du *Peri noū* d'Alexandre d'Aphrodise." Edited by J. Finnegan. *Mélange de l'Université de Saint-Josephe* 33 (1956): 157–202.

al-Fārābī, Abū Naṣr. *On the Perfect State: Abū Naṣr al-Fārābī's Mabādi' ārā' ahl al-madīnat al-fāḍilah.* Revised text with introduction, translation, and commentary by Richard Walzer. Chicago: Kazi Publications, 1998.

———. *Risala fi'l 'aql.* Edited by M. Bouyges. Beirut: Imprimerie Catholique, 1958.

Aristotle. *De Anima.* Translation, introduction, and notes by R. D. Hicks. Hildesheim: Georg Olms, 1990.

———. *Parva Naturalia.* Rome: Desclée, 1963.

———. *Selections: English & Greek; On the Soul; Parva Naturalia; On Breath.* Translated by W. S. Hett. London: W. Heinemann, 1957.

Black, Deborah. "Psychology: Soul and Intellect." In *The Cambridge Companion to Arabic Philosophy,* edited by Peter Adamson and Richard C. Taylor. Cambridge: Cambridge University Press, 2005.

Fakhry, Majid. *Al-Fārābī, Founder of Islamic Neoplatonism: His Life, Works, and Influence.* Oxford: Oneworld Publications, 2002.

Gätje, Helmut. *Studien zur Überlieferung der aristotelische Psychologie im Islam.* Heidelberg: C. Winter, 1971.

Goodman, Lenn E. *Avicenna.* London: Routledge, 1992.

Gutas, Dimitri. *Avicenna and the Aristotelian Tradition: Introduction to Reading Avicenna's Philosophical Works.* Leiden: Brill, 1988.

———. "Intuition and Thinking: The Evolving Structure of Avicenna's Epistemology." *Interdisciplinary Journal of Middle Eastern Studies* 9 (2001): 1–38.

Hasse, Dag Nikolaus. "Avicenna on Abstraction." *Interdisciplinary Journal of Middle Eastern Studies* 9 (2001): 39–73.

———. *Avicenna's De Anima in the Latin West.* London: Warburg Institute, 2000.

Ibn Rushd (Averroës). *Epitome of Parva Naturalia.* Translated from the original Arabic and the Hebrew and Latin versions with notes and introduction by Harry Blumberg. Cambridge, MA: Medieval Academy of America, 1961.

Ibn Sīnā. *Kitāb al-Najāt* [The Book of Deliverance]: *Fī al-ḥikmah al-manṭiqīyah wa-al-ṭabī'ah wa-al-ilāhīyah.* Edited by Mājid Fakhrī. Beirut: Dār al-Afāq, 1985.

Ibn Tufayl. *Ibn Tufayl's Ḥayy Ibn Yaqẓān: A Philosophical Tale.* Translated with an introduction and notes by Lenn Evan Goodman. Chicago: University of Chicago Press, 2009.

Reisman, David, and Ahmed al-Rahim, eds. *Before and After Avicenna.* Leiden: Brill, 2003.

Waugh, Earle H., and Frederick M. Denny, eds. *The Shaping of an American Islamic Discourse: A Memorial to Fazlur Rahman.* Atlanta: Scholars Press, 1998.

ENDNOTES

1. Their impact on the thought of the Jewish polymath Maimonides and the Christian writers Thomas Aquinas and Meister Eckhart is well known, but extends far beyond those often-cited examples. A remarkable testimony to that influence can be found in Samuel Ibn Tibbon's *Commentary on Ecclesiastes: The Book of the Soul of Man,* introduced and translated by James T. Robinson (Tübingen: Mohr Siebeck, 2007). In his introduction to and translation of Ibn Tibbon's commentary, Robinson elucidates the key role in the work's proemium (philosophical prelude) and in the commentary proper on Ecclesiastes. Indeed, a proemium was expected to include a disquisition on ten questions that Aristotle could have addressed more clearly, and "Aristotle" in such cases was the Aristotle as interpreted, translated, and debated within the work of philosophers like al-Fārābī, Ibn Sīnā, and Ibn Rushd. Among those questions was the debate over whether the human intellect could achieve union with the Active Intelligence; all of these, in the case of Ibn Tibbon, were issues at the heart of the book of Ecclesiastes (Kohelet) in the Hebrew Bible.

2. In their analysis of the relationship of the soul to the world of sense experience on the one hand, and to the realm of pure, immaterial intellect on the other, the Arab philosophers drew upon Aristotle's work commonly known by the Latin title *De Anima* (On the Soul, or Mind). As Rahman points out, however, the *falsafa* tradition read Aristotle's *De Anima* through the prism of commentators on Aristotle. Particularly important in this regard was the *De Anima* by the Greek writer Alexander of Aphrodisias (xv), which had been translated into Arabic and which offered a more elaborate vocabulary of the intellectual faculties and the internal senses than was presented in Aristotle's *De Anima*.

3. Throughout *Prophecy in Islam*, Rahman emphasizes both the similarities and the contrasts between the positions of al-Fārābī or Ibn Sīnā. He also notes that terminology used to depict the precise stages of intellectual formation undergoes developments and revisions within different works by the same author—particularly in the case of Avicenna, whose productivity was prodigious and who was continually refining his definitions, terms, and analysis.

4. On some occasions Rahman translated the Arabic *dhihn* as "mind" as opposed to "intellect" or "intelligence" (his choice of *ʿaql*). What the precise distinctions are between different psychological and intellectual faculties in the thought of al-Fārābī and Ibn Sīnā has generated libraries of debate.

5. Rahman, *Avicenna's Psychology*, chap. 3. Ibn Sīnā, *Kitāb al-Najāt*, ed. Fakhry, 202–5.

6. Rahman also explores the apparently contrasting positions of al-Fārābī and Ibn Sīnā on the relation of human reason to the active intelligence. In some accounts, Ibn Sīnā portrayed the active intelligence as pouring forth, or emanating, its illumination onto the lower intellects. Ibn Sīnā compared the process to the way physical sunlight allows the eye to receive the visual forms of objects and render them perceptible. The question raised in *Prophecy in Islam* (32), and vigorously debated since, is how this emanation relates to the key role played by abstraction (*tajarrud* or *intizāʿ*): that is, the progressive paring away of the corporeal aspects of forms and concepts, an operation that the human intellect carries out in cooperation with the imagination and with the active or divine intellect. See Gutas, "Intuition and Thinking," 58; and Hasse, "Avicenna on Abstraction," 39, 44–46.

7. Gutas suggests "conceptualization" as a translation for *muṣawwira*.

8. Rahman, *Avicenna's Psychology*, 35–36; Ibn Sīnā, *Kitāb al-Najāt*, 205–6.

9. Rahman, *Avicenna's Psychology*, 36; Ibn Sīnā, *Kitāb al-Najāt*, 206.

10. Rahman, *Avicenna's Psychology*, 36; Ibn Sīnā, *Kitāb al-Najāt*, 206.

11. Fazlur Rahman, "Essence and Existence in Avicenna," *Mediaeval Studies* 4 (1958): 1–16; and "Essence and Existence in Ibn Sīnā: The Myth and the Reality," *Hamdard Islamicus* 4 (1981): 3–14.

PREFACE

The purpose of this treatise is to bring into focus an area of Islamic religio-philosophical thought to which certainly not enough attention has been paid by modern scholars of Muslim thought, although Father Louis Gardet has broached the subject in his book *La Pensée Religieuse d'Avicenne* (Paris, 1951). The importance of the subject lies in the fact that it constitutes a central point at the mutual confronting of the traditional Islamic and the Hellenic thought currents. The Muslim philosophers' formulation, under the influence of Hellenism, of the doctrine of prophetic revelation—a problem at the very heart of the Muslim dogma—and the orthodoxy's reception of this doctrine, would, it is therefore hoped, help to understand the fate of Hellenism in Islam. The problem should thus be viewed in the wider setting of the inter-cultural penetration.

I have tried, so far as I have been able, to trace the Hellenic sources of the philosophical doctrine in each of its aspects. This process has revealed that the basic elements in the philosophical doctrine are all Greek, but that the Muslim philosophers have elaborated them, in some cases have refined them, and above all, have woven them, together—for the first time in the history of religious thought—in order to suit the image of the Prophet. Indeed, in order to make the traditional image intelligible to themselves, they amplified it by adding the element of intellectual perfectionism and by making it the highest of all elements. By showing how far the 'orthodoxy' accepted this image and how far it rejected it, and why, I hope the treatise will help to elucidate the very concept of orthodoxy in this respect.

In the end my thanks are due to the Editor of the Series, Prof. A. J. Arberry and Messrs George Allen & Unwin to have included a work with so many long notes and details among their publications.

F. RAHMAN
Durham
December 1957

ONE

THE DOCTRINE OF INTELLECT

The Muslim philosophers' doctrine of prophecy, so far as its psycho-logico-metaphysical bases are concerned, is founded upon Greek theories about the soul and its powers of cognition. The chief frame-work of their doctrine of the prophetic revelation is the famous doctrine of intellectual cognition obscurely mooted by Aristotle in the third book of his *De Anima*, but developed later by his commentators, especially by Alexander of Aphrodisias, although, as we shall see in the next chapter, the Muslims incorporated into this general framework, other elements, Stoic and neo-Platonic, and, above all, those found in the fluid, eclectic Hellenism of the early centuries of the Christian era.

The most important philosophical figures in Islam, who have explicitly treated the question of prophecy and have based it on the cognitive nature of the human soul, are al-Fārābī and Avicenna (Ibn Sīnā). Since, however, these two men show certain important differences in their treatment of the problem of the intellect (differ-ences, which, even if they do not seem to me to affect their doctrine of prophecy materially, are none-the-less important in themselves) and, further, employ slightly different terminology, I propose to describe their noetic doctrines separately.

I *Al-Fārābī*

According to al-Fārābī, the initial capacity, shared by all human beings and called the potential intellect, for actual intellectual cognition is not an immaterial substance but some kind of power in matter like the rest of the lower soul. So we learn that the potential intellect is 'a kind of soul or a part or a faculty of the soul or some-thing (of the kind)',[1] but, more clearly, 'the intellect possessed by a human being, naturally and from his very beginning, is some kind of disposition or preparation (hay'a) in the matter'.[2]

This potentiality or capacity is actualized in men who actually begin to acquire a knowledge of universals or forms. The actualiza-tion consists in the fact that the Active Intelligence (which according to Muslim philosphers is the last and lowest of a series of ten Intelligences emanating from God) sends out a light (an Aristotelian metaphor repeated by all his commentators) which renders the images of sensible things, stored up in man's memory, abstract and thus transforms them into intelligibles or universals. Al-Fārābī says explicitly that the forms which come to exist in the intellect or rather which the intellect becomes arise by abstraction from the sensible objects i.e. they, as such, do not flow from the Active Intelligence whose function is to render both the sensibles and the potential human intellect 'luminous'.[3] The manner in which the potential intellect receives and becomes actual intelligibles is described by al-Fārābī by the analogy of a piece of wax which receives forms not by being imprinted on its surface but by pervading its totality so that the wax is turned into an image as e.g. of a horse.[4]

When the potential intellect thus becomes one with the abstracted intelligibles and becomes actual, declares al-Fārābī, it and these intelligibles become an actual existent in the world, a new part of the intelligible furniture of reality: this he calls the 'actual intellect'. Before the potential intellect and the potential intelligibles became actual, their existence was in matter, not separate, but once actualized, they take on a new career, assume a new ontological status as a separate entity.[5] And since, he argues, every intelligible thing can be contemplated by the actual intellect by receiving its form and since the actual intellect is itself now an intelligible thing, it can therefore know itself. When thus our intellect becomes both self-intelligible and self-intellective, becomes a form of form, it becomes, in al-Fārābī's terminology, 'acquired intellect' ('aql mustafād).[6] This view of the 'aql mustafād enables al-Fārābī to go on to compare it with the Active Intelligence, since both are 'forms of form'—self intellective and self-intelligible; only, he insists, that the intelligibles contained in them are in an inverse order[7] and that the Active Intelligence is higher in rank than the mustafād, being absolutely separate[8] and containing intelligibles in a simple way, not as a plurality.[9]

Before going any further, it is worth while noting that the doctrine that once the intelligibles have been abstracted from the matter, they begin to have a new career of their own as separate and immaterial entities, is not Aristotle's or Alexander's doctrine, and this clearly sets a problem for the historian of philosophy. According to Alexander (De An, p. 85, 25 sq.), when the intelligibles have been abstracted from matter by the potential intellect, they reach a stage of *habitus* (ἕξις) where they lie in a dormant state. The intellect *in habitu* can then contemplate these intelligibles which are now no longer in matter but are in a dormant state in the mind itself. When it actually contemplates them it becomes intellect *in actu* and at this stage it can also know itself, not qua intellect but qua intelligible.[10] But Alexander says quite decidedly that these intelligibles—whether they are of material things or of mathematical objects—even when abstracted, are destructible for they have no *real* being except in individual destructible objects:[11] there is therefore no question of a new, separate career for them. Further, he seems undecided whether our intellect can know the Active Intellect or not. Sometimes he says that the human intellect *in habitu*, when it becomes operative and in action does contemplate the separate Intelligibles and becomes one with them.[12] But again we hear that the intellect in us which contemplates the Eternal Intellect comes into us from outside and is not a part of our mind. It follows that our soul is completely destructible.[13] The pseudo-Alexander, on the other hand, while affirming that the intelligibles abstracted from matter are destructible,[14] declares unequivocally that it is the human mind or our mind which can contemplate God and that by doing so it attains its utmost perfection and bliss, gaining immortality, and also becoming, like God, self-intellective.[15]

The conclusion, then, seems inescapable that although the basic framework of al-Fārābī's doctrine is that of Alexander, there are other influences at work, Platonic and, more specifically, neo-Platonic, about the status of the human mind and that of the intelligibles. The assumption, clearly, is that when the human intellect attains its proper being, it becomes self-operative, pure activity (καθαρὰ ἐνέργεια) and, correspondingly, these intelligibles, after their abstraction from matter, assume their proper status as pure intelligibles and as such are contemplated by the human intellect—both these intelligibles and the intellect being in an intermediary stage between the separate Active Intelligence and the abstracted material forms. Now this is exactly the teaching of the neo-Platonic Simplicius. According to Simplicius, the potential intellect, when actualized, returns, through the intellect *in habitu*, to its proper activity (οὐσιώδης ἐνέργεια) where it finds its proper λόγοι to contemplate and into which it is absorbed. These λόγοι, however, are not pure νοῦς but are intelligibles of the phenomenal world and in

order to become pure and indivisible intellect the human mind
has to rise one step higher.[16]

According to al-Fārābī, then, the ordinary thinking human mind
reaches its perfection when it becomes ʿaql mustafād as above described.   And, although the ʿaql mustafād is lower in rank than the
separate Active Intelligence which has produced it, it is nevertheless pure activity in its own way no longer needing the faculties of
the lower soul for its operations. It is, therefore, comparable from
this point of view with the Active Intelligence. Moreover, at this
stage, it is capable of contemplating the Active Intelligence itself
which had so far been only its productive agent.[17] In a few unique
cases, when this happens, the Active Intelligence becomes the form
of the ʿaql mustafād and the perfect philosopher, or the Imam (or
the Prophet) comes into existence.[18] Only, even in these cases, a
certain part or degree of the Active Intelligence (called the Holy
Ghost = θεῖον πνεῦμα) is involved, a part remaining completely
beyond and transcendent to man.[19] Al-Fārābī's classification of
the intellect (excluding those above the Active Intelligence) is five-
fold, as follows:—

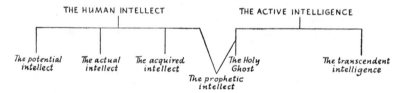

2. Avicenna (Ibn Sīnā)

According to Avicenna, the potential intellect, although it comes
into existence (and is, therefore, generated) as something personal to
each individual, is, nevertheless, an immaterial and immortal
substance.[20] Its actualization begins when man conceives the primary
general truths which are the basis of all demonstration (Aristotle's
τὰ πρῶτα, Anal. Post, I, 2, 71 b 20 sq.) e.g. that the whole is greater
than its part and that two things equal to the same thing are equal to
each other—truths, that is, which we do not acquire either by induction or by deduction.[21] This stage is called ʿaql biʾl-malaka (intell.
in habitu). When, by means of these primary truths, we acquire also
the secondary ones and when, on the whole, our mind can operate by
itself without any more help from the sensitive and imaginative

faculties, we reach the stage of development called by Avicenna the 'actual intellect' (intell. *in actu*)[22]. And when we do actually operate with this newly acquired power, our mind becomes '*aql bi'l-fiʿl al-muṭlaq* (intell. *in actu absoluto*) or '*aql mustafād* (intell. *acquisitus* or *adeptus*).[23]

For Avicenna, however, as distinguished from al-Fārābī (who in this respect holds Alexander's view), the intelligible forms which the human rational faculty receives are not produced by abstraction from matter but emanate directly from the Active Intelligence, our only antecedent manipulation being the consideration and comparing of the imaginative forms. We read in the *Shifāʾ*, *Phys. Bk.* VI, *Maqāla* 5, ch. 5: 'when the rational faculty considers the individual forms which are in the representative faculty, and is illuminated by the light of the Active Intelligence which is in us and which we have mentioned before, these imaginative (sensible) forms become abstract from matter and its attachments and are imprinted in the rational faculty *not* in the sense that the imaginative forms themselves move from the imaginative faculty into our rational faculty, nor in the sense that the intelligible shrouded in (material) attachments— while itself being abstract—produces its like (in our mind), but only in the sense that its consideration prepares the soul so that the abstract form should emanate upon it from the Active Intelligence.' Avicenna draws a qualified comparison between the 'consideratio' of the image and the conception of the premises in a syllogism, and between the emanation of the form and the emergence of the conclusion from the syllogism. The 'abstraction' of the form, therefore, for Avicenna is only a *façon de parler*.[24]

When the intellective soul becomes actually operant, it also knows itself, and its self-knowledge renders it both intellect and intelligible.[25] But Avicenna rejects the extreme interpretation, attributed by him to Porphyry, of the doctrine that the mind *becomes* the forms which it receives. It is true that the subject, in the act of knowledge, becomes its object in some sense[26] for all knowledge consists in the fact that the cognizer takes on a likeness or form of the object,[27] but it is absurd to say that the soul absolutely becomes the forms, because if it took one form and became it, it could not take on another (*Shifāʾ*, *De An* V, 6):

'The soul knows itself and this self-knowledge makes it intellect, intelligible and (actual) intellection. But its knowledge of the intelligibles does not make it so. For the soul, *so long as it subsists* in the body, is always only a potential intellect even though it becomes actual with regard to some intelligibles. The view that the soul itself becomes intelligibles is, according to me, something impossible. . . . For if this is because it discards one form and takes on another and with the first form it is one thing and with the second another thing, then the first thing does not really become the second thing, but it is destroyed and only its substratum or a part of it survives. If the soul does not become in this way then let us see how otherwise this can happen. So we say that if something becomes something else then, when it becomes that something, it itself is either existent or non-existent. If it is existent, then the second thing too (which it becomes) is either existent or not. If the second thing exists too, then there are two existents not one. But if the second thing does not exist, then the first thing has become something non-existent and not something else existent—and this is absurd. But if the first thing has become non-existent, then it has not become something else, but has ceased to exist and something else has come into existence.

'How shall the soul, then, *become* forms of things? The man who has misguided people most in this regard is the one who has composed the *Isagogy* for them. . . . True, the forms of things come to *inhere* in the soul and decorate it and the soul is like a place[28] for them, thanks to the material intellect. If the soul became the form of an actual existent, then, since the form itself, being actuality, cannot accept anything else (i.e. any other form) . . . it follows necessarily that the soul cannot accept any other form. . . . But we do in fact see that the soul accepts another form different from the one already accepted, for it would be strange indeed, if this second form does not differ from the first one, for then acceptance and non-acceptance would be the same thing'!

I have quoted this passage *in extenso* in order to show what Avicenna himself says his reasons are for denying that the soul absolutely becomes the intelligibles and what his doctrine precisely is. He says explicitly that the human *soul, so long as it is in the body,* cannot become these forms absolutely because it cannot receive them all at once and indivisibly (ἀμέριστως), and, therefore, if it became one of the forms, it could not receive another form. If it were possible for the human soul to accept all the forms at one stroke then obviously its relation to the forms would qualitatively change. Such a possibility exists, then, according to Avicenna for the soul after its separation from the body. But we see that Avicenna, not stopping even at this point, goes further and indeed declares that there may be and in fact there are human souls, namely the prophetic souls, which accept the separate intelligibles either at once or almost at once and that therefore *their* relation to these intelligibles is not the same as that of an ordinary intellect to them,[29]—_Shifā'_ (*De An* V, 6):—

'So long as the *ordinary*[30] (al-ʿāmmīya, common) human soul *remains in the body*, it is impossible for it to accept the Active Intelligence all at once . . . and when it is said that a certain person is cognizant of intelligibles (or forms), it only means that he can present in his mind a certain form when he wishes, and this means that whenever he wishes he can have some sort of contact with the Active Intelligence, so that the intelligible will be reflected (or imprinted) in his soul emanating from the Active Intelligence. . . . But when the (ordinary) human soul quits the body and its accidents, it is then possible for it to have a perfect contact (or union) with the Active Intelligence.'

The intelligibles received by the soul, according to Avicenna, cannot remain in it actually except so long as the mind actually contemplates them. The sensible forms can be conserved in the imaginative-memorative faculty, for memory is a place where these forms can be stored up when not actually used and from where they can be recalled when the deliberative mind wants to employ them again. But as regards the universal form, it cannot be placed in the memorative faculty, for then it would be a sensible, not an intelligible form. The intellect itself cannot serve as a conservatory, for the presence of the form in the intellect means actual contemplation of the form, not its conservation. And our intellectual operation being piecemeal and successive, not total, one single form cannot stay in the mind but must make room for another, or, else, the intellect would 'become' this form. Hence, for Avicenna our actual intellect is not intellect proper (κυρίως νοῦς), for proper intellect eternally thinks and becomes its object, but is rather like a mirror in which each form, emanating from the Active Intelligence, is imprinted or reflected and then withdrawn as we turn our attention to something else.[31]

The intellectual knowledge of the human soul, then, is not something simple and undivided but piecemeal and discrete where not
only is there an infinite multiplicity of propositions but even each
proposition is composed of parts, viz. subject and predicate. But
even in our ordinary cognitive experience we are aware that this
discrete mode of knowledge is not the only mode but that there is a
higher level at which the intellect is not receptive but creative.
According to Avicenna, whenever we entertain a proposition, e.g.
'every man is an animal', we are thinking in time for the order of
the concepts in a proposition also implies a time-order. The concepts making up a proposition are certainly universal and as such
can only be conceived in an immaterial substance, but the proposition
itself, since it is made up of discretely arranged concepts, is enter-
tained in time. Further, the order in which the concepts are arranged
in any given proposition, is not unique and essential, but can be
reversed: any given proposition can be translated into an equivalent
proposition in which the subject-predicate order may be reversed.
Since, however, it is not in the power of our minds to entertain
all propositions at once, it follows that the propositions we are not
actually entertaining exist not in actuality but in a state of *habitus*
or second-order potentiality. These two methods of knowledge
correspond respectively to intellect *in actu* and intellect *in habitu*.

There is, however, says Avicenna, a third mode of knowledge
which is identical with neither of these two but is regarded by him
as their creator (*Shifā, De An.* V, 6): 'An example of this is
when you are asked a question about what you have known (i.e.
in a simple manner) previously or what you are going to know soon
and so the answer presents itself to you presently. (This knowledge
consists in the fact that) you are *sure* that you will be able to answer
the question on the basis of what you already know, although there is
as yet no detail in your knowledge. On the contrary, you begin to
detail and order this knowledge in your mind when you begin to
give the answer which proceeds from an assurance that you know it,
this simple assurance being antecedent to the (ensuing) detail and
order. . . . This mode (of knowledge) is not something ordered and
explicit in your thought but is the principle of this explicit knowledge, being conjoined with an assurance. . . . If someone says
that this is only a potential knowledge but its potentiality is very near
to actuality, this is false, for the man has an actual assurance which
is not waiting to be realized through a near or remote potentiality.

The existence of this assurance means that its possessor is sure that it (i.e. the knowledge) already exists . . . . Since the actual conviction on the part of the man that the answer already lies in him must point to something actually known,[32] it is therefore already known to him in this simple manner. Then he wishes to make it known in a different way. The strange thing is that the man who answers the questions, when he begins to teach the other man the details of what has suddenly occurred to him, himself learns at the same time and acquires knowledge in the second sense. And that (simple) form begins to order and explicate itself in his mind simultaneously with the words.

'One of these two modes then is the discursive knowledge which becomes actual only by an order and a composition (of concepts), while the second is the simple knowledge which does not have successive concepts but is one and from which (successive) forms flow into their recipient (i.e. the human soul). This is the producer and principle of what we call psychic (discursive) knowledge and belongs to that absolute intellectual power of the soul which resembles the Active Intelligences. But as regards order and explicitness, they belong to the (rational) soul as such. . . . As for how does the rational soul have a principle which is not soul and which possesses a knowledge which the soul does not possess is a question deserving of thought and you must find its answer from yourself.'

Even the ordinary cognitive procedure, then, shows, according to Avicenna, the existence of a creative agency which bestows on the soul its discursive knowledge when it actually thinks. This creative power is said to be somehow in man although it is not a part of his *soul*. We shall learn in the next chapter its manner of existence in man. Now, it is this creative faculty which Avicenna calls *mustafād* (acquired),[33] since it is an emanation in man of the external Active Intelligence which is also called the Universal Intellect.[34] But we must take notice of the fact that Avicenna's terminolgy is always shifting. It is in this sense of '*aql mustafād* that Avicenna denies the identification of the ordinary human (phenomenal) soul with it and with the Active Intelligence. But he also uses the term '*aql mustafād* for these forms which flow into the human soul from this simple creative power successively and discretely: "*Aql mustafād* is really this form (i.e. which flows discretely from the creative power into the human soul); but the intellective faculty (which we possess) is the actual intellect in us in so far as *we* think. The '*aql mustafād* is the actual intellect in so far as the latter is perfected'.[35]

All these distinctions are made by Avicenna to serve as a preface for the introduction of the prophetic intellect, for the existence of a type of human intellect which, in opposition to ordinary human intelligence, can identify itself with or can 'receive' the entire Active Intelligence, thus breaking down the barrier between finite and infinite consciousness in certain special cases. Avicenna's distinctions between different intellectual levels come out as follows:—

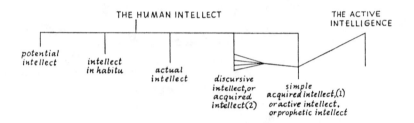

THE HUMAN INTELLECT   THE ACTIVE INTELLIGENCE

potential intellect   *intellect in habitu*   *actual intellect*   *discursive intellect, or acquired intellect(2)*   *simple acquired intellect,(1) or active intellect, or prophetic intellect*

NOTES

1. *Risāla fi'l 'Aql* (ed. M. Bouyges, Beiruth, 1938), p. 12.

2. *Al-Madīna al-Fāḍila* (ed. F. Dieterici, Leiden, 1896) p. 44, 1. This view is faithful to the teaching of Alexander of Aphrodisias (*De An*, p. 84, 24 sq.). It is true that in a treatise, *Fuṣūṣ al-Ḥikam*, attributed to him (see Chap. II, n. 32), the potential intellect is spoken of (*Philosophische Abhandlungen*, ed. F. Dieterici, Leiden, 1892, p. 76, section 43) as something immaterial and again in another treatise, *'Uyūn al-Masā'il* (*Phil. Abh.*, p. 64; this treatise was also published in Hydarābād under the name *al-da'āwī al Qalbīya* in 1349 A.H.) it is described as a simple, immaterial substance, but there are many points which raise grave doubts as to whether the attribution of these treatises to al-Fārābī is genuine. The case against their genuine authorship of al-Fārābī cannot, it seems to me, rest merely on the fact that they uphold distinction between essence and existence, for this thesis is not peculiarly Avicennian and indeed appears in other works of al-Fārābī (e.g. *Siyāsat al-Madīna*, Hydarābād, 1346 A.H.). Among the chief points to be considered are (not perhaps the fact that they are not mentioned in al-Qifṭī's list: Averroes, e.g. *De An.* Camb. Mass. 1953, p. 493 mentions a *De Gen. et Corr* by al-Fārābī, not mentioned by al-Qifṭī) that their doctrine that the passive intellect is an immaterial substance is in palpable contradiction with the teaching of both the *Madīna* and the *Fi'l–'Aql*. Again, as we shall see in the next chapter, the account given in the former treatise of the prophetic revelation and especially its teaching on the appearance of the Angel tallies completely with the account of the *Shifā'* rather than with al-Fārābī's doctrine and the description given in the same treatise (*Phil. Abh.* p. 75) of the actualization of the passive intellect as forms reflected in a mirror tallies with the teaching of the *Shifā'* and the *Ishārāt* and is not even consistent with al-Fārābī's teaching elsewhere. It is to be noted that it is only in these two treatises that a mention of the faculty of *Wahm* and the internal senses occurs whereas the *Madīna* and the *Siyāsāt* (Hydarabad, 1346, where on p. 4, 18, the perception of the harmful and the useful—the peculiar function of Wahm—is attributed to imagination, not to Wahm) e.g. are quite devoid of any such category. Averroes (*Tahāfut al-Tahāfut*, ed. Bouyges, p. 546, 1529) says that it is Avicenna alone who introduced this term. In the *'Uyūn* also occurs the term *'aql bi'l malaka* (*intellectus in habitu*) of which there is no trace either in the *Madīna* or in the *fi'l–'Aql*. It is, of course, possible that if these treatises were al-Fārābī's works, Avicenna might have followed them as, indeed, he does to a large extent, but the difficulty is that doctrines are expressed here which are not to

be found in al-Fārābī elsewhere where they could have been expected, and further, that they are *inconsistent* with what he holds elsewhere.

3. *R. fi'l–'Aql* p. 15–16; *al-Madīna al Fāḍila*, p. 45, 11:' When from the Active Intelligence there comes into the rational faculty this something which is related to the latter as light is related to (the faculty of) sight, then the sensibles, *i.e.* (Dieterici has 'an which I have read as a'nī) those ones which are stored up in the memorative (muta<u>kh</u>ayyila) faculty, emerge into the rational faculty as intelligibles.' The doctrine of abstraction, viz. that the universal emerges from successive sense-impressions accumulated in memory as 'experience' is Aristotelian (*Anal. Post*, II, 19, 100 sq.); cf. also Alex. Aphrod. *De An*, p. 83, 3 sq.: the emergence, which needs the light of the Active Intelligence, is described as a μετάβασις or a 'passing over'.

4. *R. fi'l–'Aql* p. 13–14. Aristotle (*De An*, 429 b. 30) likens the potential intellect to a tablet; Alexander insists (*De An.* p. 85, 1 sq.) that the potential intellect is not like the tablet itself but like the capacity or disposition which it possesses for receiving written words. Aristotle (*De An.* 424 a 18) cites the example of wax with regard to the sensitive faculty, but speaks only of the impression which wax receives in its surface as e.g. from a signet-ring.

5. *R. fi'l–'Aql* p. 17, 9 sq.

6. ibid p. 20, 1 (also p. 18, 9 sq.). It is clear that the *'aql mustafād* for al-Fārābī is nothing but the developed and final form of the human intellect (we shall see further on that for Avicenna it is primarily something different from the human intellect): it is not only not identified by him with the separate Active Intelligence but indeed comes into existence before it even begins to contemplate that Intelligence. Prof. E. Gilson's thesis (*Arch. d'Hist. Doctr. et Lit. du Moyen Âge*, p. 21, 10) that al-Fārābī came to identify the acquired intellect with the Active Intelligence because the Arabic translation of Alexander's *De Anima* had rendered the Greek θύραθεν by the Arabic *mustafād*, is invalidated by what al-Fārābī himself says. Further, in this translation, of which the selected Hebrew version was quoted by I. Bruns (in German) in his edition of Alexander's *De Anima*, in order to make comparison with the Greek original, even Alexander's νοῦς καθ'ἕξιν (intell. *in habitu*) appears as *mustafād* (see his *De An.*, the Hebrew version for p. 91, 3 quoted on p. 90). The development of the human intellect may come to have been called *mustafād* by al-Fārābī simply because the source of this development lies outside the potential intellect by which it is acquired. (See his *Siyāsāt*, p. 13, 4–5 where the

verb *yastafīdu* is used for its acquisition of actuality; also Alexander's *De An.*, p. 82, 1; Simpl. *De An.*, p. 236, 27 where the words ἐπικτήτως καὶ ἑτέρωθεν are used).

7. *R. fī'l-'Aql*, p. 27, 8 sq.

8. ibid, p. 21, 4–5. Al-Fārābī says that the acquired intellect is the nearest of the (sublunary) things in resemblance to the Active Intelligence (ibid, pp. 24, 8–25, 1; p. 31, 4–5), but it does not seem to be separate, despite the change wrought in the potential intellect, for, the first separate intelligence is only the Active Intelligence, and still continues to be attributed to matter (ibid, p. 24, 2–4). Thus when he says (*Madīna*, p. 46, 8–9) that the human soul becomes 'one of the things separate from bodies and one of immaterial substances' and (*R. fī'l-'Aql*, p. 31, 11–12) that the acquired intellect does not need the body for its subsistence nor a bodily organ for its operation, he probably means only that the intellect, thanks to its *habitus*, does not depend on bodily faculties and that it can, after death, have a life of its own.

9. *R. fī'l-'Aql*, p. 29, 6.

10. *De An.*, p. 86, 16 sq. In the *Mantissa* (p. 109) Alexander maintains that this intellect cannot know itself, qua intellect but only qua intelligible, since it is not a pure intellect, i.e. absolutely in act, which if it were, it would know only itself and nothing else. This is why, he says, the Active Intellect (which, according to him, is God) knows itself both qua intelligible (wherein it resembles the human intellect) and qua intellect (wherein it differs from the human intellect and is therefore simple, knowing only itself).

11. *De An.*, p. 88, 10–16; p. 90, 4 sq.

12. ibid p. 88, 5–10; p. 91, 2–4.

13. *De An.*, p. 90, 13 sq.: ὁ νοῦς ἄρα ὁ τοῦτο (i.e. the separate intellect) νοήσας ἄφθαρτός ἐστιν, οὐχ ὁ ὑποκείμενός τε καὶ ὑλικός (ἐκεῖνος μὲν γὰρ σὺν τῇ ψυχῇ, ἧς ἐστι δύναμις, φθειρομένη φθείρεται, ᾧ φθειρομένῳ συμφθείροιτο ἄν καὶ ἡ ἕξις τε καὶ ἡ δύναμις καὶ τελειότης αὐτοῦ), ἀλλ' ὁ ἐνεργείᾳ τούτῳ, ὅτε ἐνόει αὐτό, ὁ αὐτὸς γινόμενος. . . . καὶ ἔστιν οὗτος ὁ νοῦς ὁ θύραθέν τε ἐν ἡμῖν γινόμενος καὶ ἄφθαρτος.

14. Ps–Alexander, *Metaph.* p. 695, 4–7.

15. ibid., p. 698, 16 sq.; p. 714, 15 sq.

16. The most comprehensive single statement of Simplicius on the subject is *De An.* (ed. Hayduck), pp. 217, 23–221, 34. Simplicius' distinction of the intellect is five-fold: (1) the 'unparticipated intellect' which completely transcends the human soul and is God; (2) the 'intellect participated in by the soul' which is the absolute and original state of the human intellect—being indivisible—and which is the highest stage to which it returns after its escape from the material world; (3) the μένων νοῦς: this is not the indivisible intellect but is of the order of the λογικὴ ψυχή and its relation to the former is the relation of the discursive reason to the pure intuitive reason; (4) the potential intellect, which most probably, for Simplicius, is imagination (5) the intellect *in habitu* which the potential intellect becomes by the action of (3) above and then is swallowed up into it. Al-Fārābī, however, does not share Simplicius's pre-supposition that the human intellect is generated by the sinking into the body of a pure intellect which is then resurrected by degrees, even though he speaks of the hierarchy of intelligible forms in neo-Platonic terms of descent (πρόοδος) and ascent (ἐπιστροφή) cf. *R. fī'l ʿAql* p. 22. (Al-Fārābī's five-fold classification is nevertheless strikingly analogous to this form of neo-Platonism). Still more neo-Platonic is the account of Ibn Bājja (Avempache) who, in his *R. al-Ittiṣāl* (ap. Averroes' *Talkhīṣ Kitāb al-Nafs*, ed. al-Ahwānī, Cairo, 1950, p. 111), after expounding the doctrine in al-Fārābī's fashion (that the 'naturalist' first abstracts intelligibles from matter and then abstracts intelligibles from these and reaches his highest development), continues: 'Thus, man (i.e. the natural philosopher) first possesses the imaginative form . . . then the (first) intelligible form and then follows it up with the second (higher) intelligible form. This upward process . . . resembles an ascension. But if, in reality, the matter is found to be in opposite direction, it would be a descent. That is why the naturalist's contact with intelligibles represents a middle position' (cf. Simplicius' account of (3) as a μεσότης).

17. *R. fī'l–ʿAql*, p. 22, 1–2; *Madina*, p. 58, 15 sq. Averroes tells us (*De An.*, p. 433, 481, 485, 502) that al-Fārābī had not always maintained the possibility of the Active Intelligence being known by the human mind and that in his commentary on the *Nichomachean Ethics* he had argued that such a thing would involve the conclusion that a generated thing would become eternal and necessary and, further, that in adopting such a position he had expressly appealed to Alexander's opinion. It appears then that al-Fārābī had developed the doctrine of ʿaql mustafād for making possible the contact of the human mind with the Active Intelligence.

18. These terms are inter-changeable, according to al-Fārābī (*Taḥṣīl al-Saʿāda*, Hydarābād, 1345 A.H., pp. 40–43), but of this more in the next chapter.

19. cf. the distinction made by Simplicius between the 'unparticipated intellect' and the 'intellect participated in by the soul' in the last but two notes. For al-Fārābī's distinction between the two degrees of the Active Intelligence see *Siyāsāt* (Hydarābād, 1346 A.H.), p. 3, last paragraph.

20. That the potential intellect is something that comes into existence see *K. al-Najāt* (Cairo, 1938), p. 183, 13–184, 19; p. 191, 16 sq.; that it is immaterial and incorruptible, ibid., pp. 174, 20–182, 3; p. 185 sq. (see also the corresponding sections of *K. al-Shifā'*). The inconsistency of this thesis with the fundamental formula of this philosophy, viz. that either a thing is eternal and ungenerated or it is generated and corruptible, is obvious enough, but it is no doubt Avicenna's doctrine. Averroes, later on, was more consistent and declared the potential intellect to be an ungenerated substance, one for all humanity, although it connects itself with each individual.

Al-Fārābī, as we have seen, holds this intellect to be a corruptible material power, unless actualized. Consistently and boldly al-Fārābī declares that those human beings in whom this potential intellect does not become actual perish with the death of the body. In the *Madīna* (p. 67, 1) he says 'The souls of the members of ignorant (or undeveloped) societies remain unperfected and are necessarily in need of matter for their existence, because none of the primary intelligibles have been imprinted on them. So when the matter disintegrates, those faculties too disintegrate by which that which has disintegrated was sustained. . . .' See also ibid, p. 66, 20–22 and the corresponding text of the *Siyāsāt*, p. 53, 8–12 (the text of the *Siyāsāt* often closely follows—or is it vice-versa?—that of the *Madīna*). Al-Fārābī, has therefore, no doctrine of the torture after death (shaqā') but only that of the bliss (sa'āda). The doctrine, however, that not all human beings are immortal is not Islamic nor Semitic, but Greek; Diogenes Laertius (vii, 157) says that Chrysippus taught that only the souls of the Wise survived the bodily death, others perished, and Plutarch (*Plac. Phil.* 4, 7) says that whereas the souls of the uneducated were weak and disintegrated shortly after death, only those of the Wise survived until the Conflagration.

The survival of the soul, however, according to al-Fārābī, even when it has become completely independent of matter, remains individual, and Avicenna's argument for the individual survivial (*Najāt*, p. 184, 14 sq.) is taken from al-Fārābī (*Madīna*, p. 64, 8–19. In line 14, bi-mufāraqatihā is to be read as bi-muqāranatihā).

21. Aristotle nowhere states what these primary truths are. Some commentators of Aristotle later identified these first premises with the Active Intellect (see Themistius, *De An.*, p. 102, 32 sq., 189, 17 sq.). Avicenna's

examples of the primary intelligibles are identical with those of al-Fārābī (*Madīna*, p. 45, 14–15) but whereas for Avicenna these flow directly from the Active Intelligence without any manipulation on our part, for al-Fārābī these too are abstracted from matter like all other intelligibles, only they arise prior to the others and are the latter's condition.

22. *Najāt*, p. 166, 7–11 (The reading for *al-maʿqūla al-awwalīya* is to be corrected according to my *Avicenna's Psychology*, Oxford, 1952, p. 22, Ch. 4, n. 4). This stage corresponds to the νοῦς καθ' ἕξιν of Alexander of Aphrodisias following whom Avicenna describes this new intellectual power as a treasure in which intelligibles lie buried or dormant.

23. Ibid, p. 166, 12 sq., this corresponds to the νοῦς κατ' ἐνέργειαν of Alexander.

24. This account, apparently not that of Aristotle, Alexander or al-Fārābī, would be quite at home in the neo-Platonic climate, cf., e.g. the account given above of Simplicius' doctrine of the intellect according to which the λόγοι are not really abstracted from matter but are bestowed on the potential intellect by the higher intellectual being which is not immersed in matter and which by doing so ressurrects the potential intellect from matter into its proper being. This general procedure, which Simplicius designates by the term ἐγείρεσθαι 'to be awakened or re-surrected', is applied by him also to sense-perception and is, indeed, a universal characterizing feature of the neo-Platonic doctrine of all know-ledge. We thus see that whereas al-Fārābī is a peripatetic in respect of the *genesis* of intelligible forms but is neo-platonic as regards the *status* of these forms, the reverse is the case with Avicenna. From these and similar other considerations it emerges that it is not free from danger to characterize generally the individual Muslim Philopsophers and to say, e.g. that al-Fārābī is more Aristotelian while Avicenna is more neo-Platonic.

25. For Alexander, as we have seen, the human mind when *in habitu* becomes an intelligible (νοητόν), by identifying itself with its objects, but it never becomes intellect (νοῦς). Simplicius, however, rejects (*De An.*, p. 230, 12 sq.) Alexander's view and says that the mind knows itself qua itself not as being identical with its objects.

26. *Najāt*, p. 246, 2. So Alexander of Aphrodisias (*De An.*, p. 91, 20–21): ἑκάστοτε μέν. . . . πως γίνεται (note the qualification πως).

27. The doctrine that the knower becomes the known object in the sense that it becomes like it (ὁμοιοῦσθαι) is universal Greek doctrine of cognition

after Aristotle. But this admits of varying degrees. Thus Alexander (*De An.*, p. 84, 2–88, 16) distinguishes between (1) the sense in which a material object becomes like another, (2) that in which the sentient becomes like the sensatum, (3) that in which the intellect becomes like the intelligibles which it abstracts, and (4) that in which the intellect becomes like the *per se* intelligible. Often, however, a simple 'becoming' is substituted for 'becoming like' and the highest form of this 'becoming' in man is when he knows God. It is, therefore, somewhat arbitrary when P. Louis Gardet (*La Pensée Religieuse D'Avicenne*, Paris, 1951, pp. 156–7) insists on a fundamental and sharp distinction between the peripatetic doctrine which he calls a purely 'psychological' unity or becoming and the neo-Platonic which he terms an 'ontological' unity or becoming. For it was Aristotle who taught (*Met.* XII, 7, 1072b, 14) that when knowing God, we temporarily live and share Divine life.

28. cf. Aristotle's description of the soul as a 'place of forms' (*De An.*, III, 429 a, 27).

29. For the reasons outlined here, it seems to me that Pére L. Gardet's account of the subject (op. cit. pp. 153–7) is not merely extrinsic but out of harmony with Avicenna's own teaching. Gardet's belaboured argument tries to establish that Avicenna denied the identity of the human soul with the separate intelligibles in the cognitive act because he did not wish to identify the human soul with God in higher religious experience. He says (p. 155, 3–6) 'c'est bien la theorie de la connaissance qui est en jeu. Cela vaut-il contre une union mystique qui serait totale fusion? Certes, dês la que chez Avicenne la connaissance mystique sera de meme mode que toute connaissance intellectuelle.' This is a result of the general policy of Gardet in the book to show that Avicenna was anxious to keep his fidelity to traditional Islam and indeed that he tried to integrate the *entire* traditional Islam with his philosophy. We shall say something about this in Section IV of the 2nd chapter. As for this subject, it is clear that Avicenna denies the identity of the intellect and the intelligible only in so far as the soul is in the body and even while in the body *some* souls may have, according to him, perfect, total contact with the Active Intelligence. The reason, he gives is that the ordinary human soul, while in the body, must receive these forms in succession and piecemeal.

For Avicenna, there cannot, of course, be a total mergence of the human personality in God (or, more strictly, in the Active Intelligence) since, both for him and for al-Fārābī, the human survival is individual and personal. And this shows that the doctrine of the intellect's *becoming* its object or not is a philosophical doctrine of cognition and not so much a religious doctrine. It is, however, impossible to keep a sharp distinction between the two. If P. Gardet were right, why should Avicenna allow the identity of the intellect and the intelligible in the case of the prophets, of the disembodied souls and, indeed, of the separate Intelligences? P. Gardet also tries to prove that there has been a real development in Avicenna's thought on the subject and he regards the *Isharāt* as the final, developed statement of his position. Yet, we find in the *Isharāt* (Cairo, 1948, Vol. III, p. 217) the following: 'when (after God) all being is reflected in it (i.e. in the intellect) . . . in such a manner that it does not remain distinct from the (knowing) substance'; and we find (ibid., Vol. II, pp. 421–39) a long (and unprobative) argument to establish the intellect —intelligible identity in the separate Intelligences. But these Intelligences do not apparently become identical with God.

30. The ordinary human soul here obviously means the philosophical mind of which, as we shall see later, the highest point is reached in a mystic contemplation, but which is to be radically distinguished from the prophetic mind.

31. This way of representing the matter does not seem to be peripatetic. In the next chapter we shall try to show how it could have arisen. For the present it must suffice to quote a passage from Plutarch (*De Genio Socratis*, XXII): τὸ μὲν οὖν ὑποβρύχον ἐν τῷ σώματι φερόμενον ψυχὴ λέγεται·τὸ δὲ φθορᾶς λειφθ ἐν, οἱ πολλοὶ Νοῦν καλοῦντες, ἐντὸς εἶναι νομίζουσιν αὐτῶν, ὥσπερ ἐν τοῖς ἐσόπτροις τὰ φαινόμενα κατ᾽ ἀνταύγειαν· οἱ δέ ὀρθῶς ὑπονοοῦντες ὡς ἐκτὸς ὄντα, Δαίμονα προσαγορεύουσι. According to this passage, intellect proper remains outside the phenomenal man, although some people inappropriately designate intellect what is nothing more than a reflection in a mirror in the soul of man.

32. i.e. Conviction is not a purely psychological occurrence in a mind but implies a relation and as such presupposes something of which the subject is convinced, and this something in this sense is already known. An illustration of this doctrine could be what is known as the 'professional confidence' acquired through the learning and exercise of a special skill or art (e.g. the art of medicine) on the analogy of which the doctrine of the intellect is based and developed both by Aristotle and his commentators and Avicenna himself. But obviously Avicenna's doctrine of confidence is not restricted to an acquired skill but is intended for a much wider use. Indeed, this confidence, according to him, owes its being not to the learning of a skill as such but to the presence of a simple, creative knowledge which grants us a 'psychic', discursive knowledge.

Certainty and assurance, it should be noted, do not by themselves constitute knowledge; the point is that they could not occur without the presence of some simple and creative form of knowledge from which proceeds 'scientific' knowledge. The emphasis on certainty and conviction is of course of Stoic origin; for the Stoics certainty was a kind of knowledge: ἄλλην δὲ (ἐπιστήμην) ἕξιν φαντασιῶν (εἶναι) δεκτικήν ἀμετάπτωτον ὑπὸ λόγου ἥντινα φασιν ἐν τόνῳ καὶ δυνάμει (τῆς ψυχῆς) κεῖσθαι (Stobaeus, Ecl., II, 128). Nevertheless, Avicenna's theory has obviously a very different orientation from the Stoic one, for here certainty is creative of knowledge and not something attached to it in the mind as a criterion of its truth, although the fact, that the Stoics could call this mere mental attitude knowledge, is significant. It seems that this Stoic doctrine of certainty in relation to knowledge played a progressively increasing part in the early Christian centuries as Stoicism came to be blended more and more with Platonism (and neo-Pythagoreanism). In one direction it led to the Ciceronian-Stoic doctrine of the immediate certainty of all knowledge based on the notion of the *inchoatae* or *adumbratae intelligentiae*.

The other direction, more closely akin to Avicenna's theory of knowledge, is the doctrine of the Hermetists. According to this doctrine, the soul which aspires to *gnosis* must initially possess a disposition which the Hermetists describe by the terms δύναμις and πίστις. See especially *Hermetica* (ed. W. Scott, Vol. 1) libellus XI, ii, 20b–21b, where great emphasis is laid on this δύναμις and confidence as a pre-requisite of all knowledge: τό δέ δύνασθαι γνῶναι . . . καὶ ἐλπίσαι ὁδός ἐστιν εὐθή . . . etc. According to the same doctrine, however, this πίστις or confidence already implies some form of knowledge: only an ἔννους can have πίστις (op. cit. lib. X, 10), and in lib. IV, 11b this state of mind is described as an eye of the mind (ὁ καρδίας ὀφθαλμός) or an insight which itself leads to knowledge (cf. Augustine's famous doctrine: credimus ut cognoscamus).

The formal characteristics of Avicenna's doctrine are therefore Stoic-Hermetic. The *content* of the doctrine, however, viz. that the discursive knowledge is preceded by a simple, total creative knowledge is more explicitly a Plotinian doctrine. See below, chap. II, note 2.

33. See *R. fi ithbāt al-nubuwwāt* in *Tis' Rasā'il* (Cairo, 1908), p. 122, 12.

34. op. cit. (p. 122, 1) this *mustafād* is also called the Active Intelligence or the Active Intellect. Actually, the acquired intellect is nothing but the Active Intelligence in so far as it projects itself into man.

35. *Shifā'* (*De An.*, V, 6). It is also abundantly clear that in whatever Avicennian sense of the '*aql mustafād* we use the term, it is radically different from the '*aql mustafād* of al-Fārābī.

PROPHECY

I *The Intellectual Revelation*

Avicenna's doctrine of the intellect has introduced us, even in ordinary cognitive experience,[1] to a form of knowledge where the soul begins to receive knowledge from above instead of looking for it to the 'natural' world below it, or rather, where the soul receives a power whereby it creates knowledge. This power or faculty which creates knowledge in the soul, is not a part of the soul itself, and is regarded as a form of knowledge since it is accompanied by a strong assurance and certainty and, further, as a higher and simpler mode of cognition, since it creates the detailed and discursive knowledge in the soul.[2]

The prophet, then, is a person of extraordinary intellectual endowment such that, by means of it, he is able to know all things by himself without the help of instruction by an external source.[3] Although both al-Fārābī and Avicenna agree in this, al-Fārābī nevertheless seems to deem it necessary that the prophetic illumination or revelation be preceded by ordinary philosophic thinking: the prophet's intellect should go through the stages of development through which an ordinary thinking mind passes; and only then the revelation comes, the only difference between the prophetic and the ordinary person being that the former is self-taught:—

'The absolutely first chief (of the good state) is the one who is not directed by any other man in anything. On the contrary, he has actually attained all knowledge and gnosis (by himself) and he is not in need of anyone to direct him in any matter. . . . This happens only in the case of a man who is endowed with exceptionally great natural capacities when his soul attains contact with the Active Intelligence. This stage is reached only after this man has first achieved the actual intellect[4] and then the acquired intellect. For it is by the attainment of the acquired intellect that a contact with the Active Intelligence is achieved as has been shown in the book on the soul.[5] It is this man who is really the King according to the ancients and it is about him that it is said that revelation comes to him.

Revelation comes to a man when he has reached this rank, i.e. when no intermediary remains between him and the Active Intelligence. Thus, the actual intellect is like matter and substratum unto the acquired intellect which itself is like matter and substratum unto the Active Intelligence.'[6]

This is all that is to be found in al-Fārābī's extant treatises about the prophetic revelation at the intellectual level. The three points made by him are (1) that the prophet, unlike an ordinary mind, is endowed with an extraordinary intellectual gift, (2) that the prophet's intellect, unlike ordinary philosophical and mystical minds, does not need an external instructor but develops by itself with the aid of divine power even if, previous to its final illumination, it passes through the stages of actualization, through which an ordinary intellect passes, and (3) that, at the end, of this development the prophetic intellect attains contact with the Active Intelligence from which it receives the specifically prophetic faculty.[7]

Avicenna has taken up in his doctrine the Fārābian basis, but has modified and developed it in a fuller account of the intellectual revelation. For him too the prophetic mind does not need external instruction, but he conceives of the prophetic revelation not as occurring at the end of a noetic development but as something sudden, happening with a *coup*. In order to show the possibility of such a form of cognition, he constructs a doctrine of intuition based essentially on the Aristotelian concept of ἀγχίνοια but as developed by the Stoics in relation to their doctrine of the revelation of the wise man. We know, Avicenna tells us,[8] that people differ in their power of intuition, i.e. hitting at a truth without consciously formulating a syllogism in their minds and therefore without time. Since there are people who are almost devoid of this power, while there are others who possess it, again, some in greater others in lesser degree, it follows that there may be a man naturally so gifted that he intuits all things at a stroke or 'flares up'[9] with an intuitive illumination, as Avicenna puts it. The Active Intelligence deposits the forms of all things, past, present and future into the prophet's soul and Avicenna adds that this deposition is not a mere irrational acceptance on the part of the prophet but has a rational order of cause and effect 'for a mere acceptance (as of chance happenings, as it were) in the realm of things which are known only through their causes does not possess certainty and rationality.'[10]

All intellectual knowledge, according to Avicenna, comes from the Active Intelligence and not from perceptual experience, as we saw in the last chapter. But there are two ways in which the prophetic intellect differs from ordinary philosophical or mystical cognition. In the first place, the ordinary mind has first to exercise itself on the data of perceptual experience. This is because the human mind is like a mirror or like an eye. This mirror, in an ordinary person, is rusty, through its contact with the body, or this eye is diseased. In this case the sensitive and cogitative processes are necessary which constitute the polishing of the mirror or the treatment of the eye. But in the case of the prophetic mind this is not necessary since it is by nature pure and can therefore directly contact the Active Intelligence:—

'(The prophetic intellect) possesses a strong capacity for this (i.e. for contact with the Active Intelligence) as though it already possesses the second capacity (i.e. the intellect *in habitu*), nay, as though it knows everything from within itself. This degree is the highest point of this capacity and this state of the material intellect should be called Divine Intellect. It is of the kind of the intellect *in habitu* except that it is of a very high order and not all human beings partake of it' (*Najāt*, p. 167, 2–5).

Secondly—and Avicenna is most insistent on this—the ordinary mind, even when it has risen to intellectual cognition, receives intelligibles only partially and one after another: one reflection has to be removed from the mirror in order to give place to the succeeding one. The prophet's mind, on the other hand, receives all knowledge at once.

Why is this difference between the prophetic and the ordinary intellect? This is a major problem for Avicenna's higher or religious epistemology, but it is also a problem to which he has left no clear answer. We should be getting nearer to giving an answer, if we knew the nature of the Active Intelligence and its precise relation to the human mind, a question which Avicenna has raised in the *Shifā* (*Phys*. VI, 5, 6) but which he has made no direct attempt to solve anywhere:—

'This creative knowledge (i.e. the active intellect) belongs to the absolutely noetic *faculty of the soul* resembling the (external)

Active Intelligences, whereas the explication and detail belong to the *soul* as such so that one who does not possess this latter kind of knowledge, does not possess psychic knowledge. As to how the rational soul has a principle which is other than the soul itself and which has a knowledge different from that of the soul, is a difficult question and you must try to understand this by yourself.'

In fact, the doctrine of the certainty and of the immediate and direct quality of intuitive religious cognition demands that the creative principle of knowledge be in the mind as a part of it and Avicenna indeed calls it in the above quotation as a part or faculty of the rational human soul. On the other hand, the scruple, that if it is a part of the soul then all men should equally participate in it, and the scruple of absolutely identifying the Giver of Revelation—the directive principle of humanity—with man himself, tend towards externalizing and transcendentalizing it. Both these tendencies appear in the following passage which is the most detailed on this subject Avicenna has left us:—

'(The human soul, besides the material intellect and the intellect *in habitu*) has a third faculty (*wa* should be read for *aw* in the last line of p. 121) which is (already) "informed" with the forms of actual universal intelligibles and by which the previous two faculties (i.e. the material intellect and the intell. *in habitu*) were (*wa* to be omitted) actualized (al-fiʻl to be read for al-ʻaql): this is called the Active Intellect.

'The Active Intellect does not actually exist in the material intellect; hence it does not exist in the latter essentially and therefore it comes to exist in it from (another) which gives it and in which it exists essentially and through which (ultimately) the potential (intellect) was actualized: this is called the Universal Intellect, the Universal Soul or the World Soul[12].

'Now since everything that essentially receives a faculty receives it in two ways, viz., indirectly or directly, similarly, (*wa* should be omitted) reception (by the human soul) from the Universal Active Intelligence is in two modes: either directly, as the reception of common notions and self-evident truths,[13] or indirectly, as the reception of secondary intelligibles through instruments and material things like external sense, *sensus communis*, the estimative faculty and the imaginative-deliberative faculty.

B

'Now since, as we have shown, the rational soul sometimes receives (knowledge) indirectly and sometimes directly, it follows that it does not possess direct reception essentially but accidentally. Essential direct reception is then in something else which is acquired[14] and which is the Angelic Intellect possessing essential direct reception. . . .

'Next, we notice that both the receiver and the received are of varying degrees as regards strength and weakness, of facility and difficulty. Now it is impossible that this should not have its ultimate limits: the limit on the side of weakness is that (a human soul) cannot accept even a single intelligible either directly or indirectly while the limit on the side of strength is that (a human soul) should accept (all knowledge) directly. . . .

'Now we have made clear (elsewhere) that when something is a composite of two notions and one of the two is found by itself, the other also must be found (i.e. must exist) by itself. We have (thus) seen that there are things (i.e. human beings) which accept both directly and indirectly, others which do not accept directly any emanation from the (Active) Intellect, others again which directly receive all intelligible emanations. . . .

'This (last type) is called the prophet and to him belongs the ultimate limit of excellence in the realm of material forms. And since that which excels is ruler over that which it excels, the prophet is the ruler over all the species which he excels.

'Revelation is this emanation (from the Universal Intellect into the prophet's soul) and the Angel is this (extra) faculty or power[15] received (by the prophet as a part of his nature) and emanation (from the Active Intelligence) as if it emanates into the prophet being continuous with the Universal Intelligence, flowing from it not essentially but accidentally'.[16]

In the words 'The Angel is this (extra) faculty or power received (by the prophet i.e. as a part of his nature) and emanating (from the Active Intelligence) as if it emanates into the prophet being continuous with the Universal (Active) Intelligence, *flowing from it not essentially* but accidentally' we have a clue to the understanding of the relation between the prophet and the Active Intellect. The words 'not essentially but accidentally' convey here the same meaning as they do in the celebrated Avicennian doctrine of existence as an 'accident'. Just as in that doctrine, not all conceivable essences exist but some do exist, and so existence is regarded as something extra in relation to the essence, although not as an extra element in the individual existent, so here, since not all human beings receive the creative prophetic faculty but some rare exceptions do, it is regarded as something extra to humanity as such although not extra to the individual prophet. It follows that the Active Intellect, although being a supernal reality to humanity, is a part and parcel of the prophet qua prophet: phenomenally speaking, the prophet as human being, is not the Active Intellect but since in his case the barrier between the phenomenal and the ideal (real) has broken down, he is identical with the Active Intellect.

We are now able to understand better the difference between the ordinary rational consciouness and the prophetic consciousness. The ordinary consciousness is, for the most part, receptive, not creative and receives piecemeally what the Active Intellect creates as a totality. In the Avicennian phrase, quoted in Chapter I, the ordinary mind has only reflections in the mirror, not real, veritable knowledge which can be possessed only when man's phenomenal self unites itself with the Ideal personality, the Angelic Intellect.[17] Hence the prophet is described as possessing Divine Intellect, Divine Pneuma, and as a Divine Being, deserving of honours and almost to be worshipped (cf. the last words of the *Shifā'*) because he 'accidentally' (i.e. not qua an 'ordinary' human being) receives in himself the Angelic Intellect, the Daimon.[18]

As has been said before, the Muslim philosophers do not seem to recognize the technical prophecy or prophecy by rational conjecture, esteemed by Hellenism. With Plato, Plutarch, Plotinus and others they admit a highest flight of the human soul by which it gains a simple, total insight into Reality; with Plotinus they agree that this insight is creative of discursive rational knowledge comprising premises and conclusions which, according to them, correspond with causes and effects since they agree with the Stoics[19] that every event has its fixed place in a stringent and unalterable causal scheme. They would, therefore, not quarrel about the names by which such a man is to be called—Prophet, Mystic or Philosopher, for, at the highest point they are all one at the intellectual level, although the prophet is distinguished especially by the Technical Revelation which we shall consider in the next section and by the moral and legal socio-political mission which we shall discuss in the last section.[20]

Not however, every mystic or philosopher is Mystic, Philosopher

or Prophet. There are innumerable grades according to the innumerable differences in natural capacities of men. What we have described
is the highest pinnacle of Wisdom not attainable by everyone and
the true Sage or Prophet is a very rare occurence in the world.[21]

II *The Technical or Imaginative Revelation*

If at the intellectual level the prophet, the philosopher and the
mystic are identical, the prophet is distinguished from the others
by a strong imaginative faculty. The central principle on which
the Muslim philosophers found their explanation of the inner,
psychological processes of technical revelation is that the imaginative faculty represents in the form of particular, sensible images
and verbal modes, the universal simple truth grasped by the prophet's
intellect.[22]

This principle, employed and explained at length by al-Fārābī,
was taken over by Avicenna. But Avicenna has added to this another
account, largely as a supplement, namely, the influx of certain
images into the soul through the influence of the heavenly bodies.
As we shall see further on, this theory was introduced by Avicenna
to characterize an inspiration (ilhām) which is different from and
lower than the prophetic revelation (waḥy).

Figurization and symbolization is a function peculiar to the
imaginative faculty. Every datum, whether it is intellectual or
sensible or emotional, imagination transforms into vivid and potent
symbols capable of impelling to action. If, e.g. our appetitive faculty
is in a state of preparedness, say, towards pleasure, but is not strong
enough to move the organism, the imaginative faculty often stirs
up lively symbols and images of pleasure so that they move the
organism. And further, even if our emotional and appetitive soul is
not in a state of readiness towards any object of pleasure but our
purely physiological condition is conducive to it, the imaginative
faculty can, by presenting suitable images, bring the emotion itself
into action and move the organism. Both al-Fārābī and Avicenna
cite as an example the fact that imagination can stir up sexual appe-
tite by suggesting suitable images to the mind.[23]

What we are, however, concerned with at present is the figurization of religious intellectual truth. Now imagination must necessarily
express this truth in figurative language since, not being an immaterial faculty, it cannot grasp the universal and the immaterial.[24]

But imagination cannot always perform this function because in ordinary waking life it is engaged as an intermediary between the perceptual and the intellectual faculties: it receives sensual images from the former, acts upon them by division and combination, and places them at the service of the mind for practical needs of life.[25] When, however, in sleep, the soul withdraws from the sensible world and no longer performs this funtion for the mind, it assumes its proper function freely.[26]

But if in the case of ordinary human beings, the withdrawal of the soul takes place only in dreams, in the case of rare exceptions who are endowed with a pure soul and a strong imagination, this can happen also in waking life:—[27]

'. . . When the imaginative faculty is very strong and perfect in a man and neither the sensations coming from the external world, nor its services to the rational soul, overpower it to the point of engaging it utterly—on the contrary, despite this engagement, it has a superfluity of strength which enables it to perform its proper function—its condition with all its engagements in waking life is like (other men's souls') condition when they are disengaged in sleep. Under such circumstances, the imaginative soul figurizes the intelligibles bestowed upon it by the Active Intelligence in terms of perceptual (literally: visible) symbols. These figurative images, in their turn, impress themselves on the perceptual faculty.

'Now, when these impressions come to exist in the *sensus communis*, the visual faculty is affected by them and receives their impress. These impressions are then transmitted through the visual ray to the surrounding air filled with light and when they thus come to exist in the air, they come back and impinge upon the visual faculty in the eye and are transmitted back to the imagination through the *sensus communis*.

'Since this entire process is inter-connected, what the Active Intelligence had originally given to this man (in terms of intelligibles) thus comes to be perceptually apprehended by him. In cases where the imaginative faculty had symbolized these truths with sensible images of utmost beauty and perfection, the man who comes to see them exclaims "Verily! God has overwhelming majesty and greatness; what I have witnessed is something wonderful not to be found in the entire range of existence".

'It is not impossible that when a man's imaginative power reaches

extreme perfection so that he receives in his waking life from the
Active Intelligence a knowledge of present and future facts or of their
sensible symbols and also receives the symbols of immaterial intelligibles and of the higher immaterial existents and, indeed, sees
all these—it is not impossible that he becomes a prophet giving news
of the Divine Realm, thanks to the intelligibles he has received. This
is the highest degree of perfection a man can reach with his imaginative powers.'[29]

Avicenna has taken over this doctrine of the visual and acoustic
symbolization, by imagination, of the intellectual phenomena.[30] But
he seems to regard the appearance of the angel and the hearing of the
angel's voice as purely mental phenomena[31] unlike al-Fārābī who,
as the above quotation shows, regards them as veritable perceptions
(even though, most probably, as being private to the prophet and not
'objective' in the accepted sense of that word) having their counter-
parts in the occurrences of the external world (light, air etc.) and
the perceptual organs of the experient.

The points that have emerged so far are (1) that the prophet is
endowed with such a strong power of imagination that he can re-
capture the intellectual truth by figurization in visual and acoustic
symbols in waking life and (2) that although these symbols may be
private and not public, this fact does not interfere with their objective
validity. The truth of this last statement would be guaranteed by
the fact that the ultimate source of the truth, the intellectual inspiration, which the symbols embody, occurs at a level from which the
possibility of falsehood or error is *ex hypothesi* excluded and therefore
it does not matter whether the symbols are subjective or objective.[32]

Besides this figurizing activity of the imagination, in which
purely intellectual truth appears in perceptual form, Avicenna admits
the influence which the imagination of the heavenly bodies exercises
on, not only the earthly bodies, but also the human souls.[33] Knowledge gained in this manner chiefly relates to future events. This kind
of prophecy is made possible by the fact that the souls of the heavenly
bodies turn into discrete individual images the universal decree of
God transmitted to them through the separate intelligences—much
after the manner of the human soul—and these images then flow into
the human souls.[34]

Why does Avicenna introduce this second line of fore-knowledge
since the first type of knowledge seems adequate to explain all fore-

knowledge of the future? It seems from the heading, *Najāt*, p. 299
and from p. 301 that he wished to draw thereby a distinction between
the prophecy of the prophets and the prophetic activity (ilhām) sometimes exercised by other people, like mystics. It is also clear that an
ordinary mystic does not possess the former kind of prophecy whereby
a verbal revelation is received and a religious law instituted, thanks
to the emanation of intellectual truth into the imaginative faculty.

In any case, whether the prophet's imagination figurizes the
intellectual and spiritual truth or it receives particular images from
the heavenly bodies, it cannot usually represent the *naked* truth since it
is ever prone to symbolization by association of images:—'A function
of this imaginative faculty is that it is always busy with the store-
houses of external and internal images. . . . When it begins with a
given external or internal image, it moves on to its contrary or to
something similar or to something which is its cause (or to which it
is somehow related), for this is its very nature. There are innumerable
particular reasons as to why in specific cases it moves from one
thing either to its contrary and not to something similar or vice
versa. The fundamental principle, however, in all this must be that
whenever the soul considers internal and external images together, it
moves from an internal image to an external one which is close to it
either absolutely or because of their contiguity which they gain from
perceptual or imaginative association, and so from an external
image to an internal one. . . .

'And you should know that rational deliberation has to labour hard
to cope with this faculty and its ever treacherous behaviour. For,
whenever reason employs it in the direction of a certain object, it
quickly moves on to something else not (essentially) connected with
the former and thence again to something else, so that the mind for-
gets what it started with until it is forced to recollect by a reverse
analytic process. . . .

'When in waking hours the soul happens to perceive something (of
the unseen world) or contact the Angelic Realm in sleep, as we shall
describe later, if the imaginative faculty is restful or overpowered,[35]
it enables it (i.e. the soul) to record well . . . in its memory the form
as it appears, so that it neither needs recollection if (this vision)
takes place in waking hours, nor interpretation if it is a dream, nor
again allegorical interpretation if it is a case of revelation, for in
the last two cases interpretation and allegorization take the place

of recollection. . . . In any case, that form of vision in which the imagination holds sway always needs to be interpreted.'[36]

Besides, however, this inner compulsion of what we may call the Psychological Law of Symbolization, there appears another account of Technical Revelation which one might call political (in the wider sense of the word): it says that since the masses cannot grasp the purely spiritual truth, the prophets communicate this truth to them in materialistic symbols and metaphors.[37] This account is abundantly found among the Muslim philosophers but especially in al-Fārābī who seems to have concerned himself with politio-social philosophy more than the rest:—

'Either a man rationally conceives the principles of existence and their ranks, the salvation and the government of good states, or understands them only figuratively. Their rational conception is that their essences impress themselves upon the (rational) soul of man, just as they are; their imaginative understanding is that their images and symbols impress themselves upon the soul. . . .

'Most men are unable—either by nature or by custom—to understand these things by rational conception. These men should be furnished with imaginative symbols of the principles of existence and their ranks, the Active Intelligence and the Primary Rulership (i.e. prophecy). Now, the essences of these things are one (among all nations) and unchangeable, but their symbols are many and different, some nearer to the essence, some further removed. This is analogous to the case of visibles: the image of a visible man in water, e.g. is nearer to the real man than the image in water of the statue of the same man.

'Therefore, the symbols of these realities current in one people differ from those current in another, and so the religions even of good societies and states come to differ, even though they all believe in an identical type of salvation (or happiness), since religion is only the imaginative symbols in the minds of a people. For, since the masses cannot understand these things in their real existence, attempts are made to teach them in other ways, viz. those of symbolism.

'These things are thus allegorized for every nation or people in terms familiar to them, and it is possible that what is familiar to one people is foreign to another. Most people who believe in happiness can believe in it only in figurative, not conceptual terms.

Those people who believe in happiness because they can rationally conceive it and receive (the essence) of the principles, are the Sages (ḥukamā'), whereas those who figuratively understand them and believe in them as such (i.e. who believe the figurative truth to be literal truth) are the Believers.'[38]

Positive religions, then, are pragmatic movements instituted either by God for the whole of humanity including the prophets, if these latter are themselves subject to belief in the religious symbols (as well as in the higher truth), thanks to the compulsory Psychological Law of Symbolization, or by the prophets for the rest of humanity, if only the political approach to the genesis of religions is admitted. But they are not entirely so, for each great religion, at any rate, contains, in its corpus of revelations, sufficient glimpses of pure truth to lead the elect seekers of truth to pursue this truth itself and to be able to allegorically interpret the rest of the symbols.[39]

The spiritual content and background of all religion is identical, as it appears from the foregoing quotation of al-Fārābī, since this is universal,[40] but it is equally true that the symbols in which positive religions have expressed (or hidden?) this truth are not at the same level. Some are nearer the truth than others, some are more adequate than others in leading humanity to the higher truth, some, again, are more effective than others in gaining the belief of people and becoming the directive force of their lives. Indeed, there are religions whose symbolisms are positively harmful:—

'The images which symbolize these (higher truths) differ in merit: some are more firm and adequate in their imagery, others are less so; some are nearer to the truth, others less so; in some the objectionable or controversial points (mawādiʿ al- ʿinād) are either few or less apparent or are such that it is not easy to object to them; others the contrary of these. . . . If the symbols are essentially equivalent in the excellence of their symbolization or in having the least number of objectionable points and in the fact that these are least apparent, then all of these symbolic-systems may be used or whichever of these happens to be more convenient (for other reasons). But if these symbolic-systems differ in rank, then that one should be chosen which is most adequately symbolic and in which there are no objectionable points at all, or are very few and unapparent . . . others must be rejected.'[41]

B*

Religious symbols, if they are to be properly understood, must be interpreted,[42], as has been said above. But this interpretation can be only for the sake of a few who are possessed of sufficient intelligence to understand it; for the mass of dullards the letter of the revelation and the materialistic symbols must remain the literal truth.[43] This doctrine is very common among the Muslim philosophers. Averroes, in his *Faṣl-al-Maqāl* (Cairo, 1317 A.H., pp. 18, 29) accuses al-<u>Ghazālī</u> of trying to divulge the esoteric meaning of the Sacred Books and of having fallen between two stools. In the *Tahāfut al-Tahāfut* (p. 584) he declares that a religion based purely on reason must always be inferior to Revealed Religions which are based both on reason and imaginative symbolization. But perhaps nobody has expounded this thesis more strongly than Avicenna who fervently, almost passionately, holds that if a person speaks the bare truth to the public, his message must be considered to be devoid of divine origin (cf. n. 41 above) and that the symbols must remain the literal truth for the largest part of humanity. I quote below the relevant part of his *Risāla al-Aḍḥawīya* (pp. 44, 10–51, 5):—

'As for religious law, one general principle is to be admitted, viz. that religions and religious laws, promulgated through a prophet, aim at addressing the masses as a whole. Now, it is obvious that the deeper truths concerning the real Unity (of God), viz. that there is one Maker (of the Universe) who is exalted above quantity, quality, place, time, position and change, which lead to the belief that God is one without anyone to share His species, nor is He made of parts— quantitative or conceptual—that neither is He transcendent nor immanent, nor can He be pointed to as being anywhere—it is obvious that these deeper truths cannot be communicated to the multitude. For if this had been communicated in its true form to the bedouin Arabs or the crude Hebrews, they would have refused straightway to believe and would have unanimously proclaimed that the belief to which they were being invited was belief in an absolute nonentity.

'This is why the whole account of the Unity (of God) in religion is in anthropomorphisms. The Koran does not contain even a hint to (the deeper truth about) this important problem,[44] nor a detailed account concerning even the obvious matters needed about the doctrine of the Unity, for a part of the account is apparently anthropomorphic while the other part contains absolute transcendence (i.e. total unlikeness of God to His creation) but in general terms, without specification or detail.[45] The anthropomorphic phrases are innumerable but they (i.e. the orthodox interpreters of the Koran) do not accept them (as they stand). If this is the position concerning the Unity, what of the less important matters of belief?[46]

'Some people may say: "Arabic language allows latitudinarian use and metaphorism; anthropomorphisms like the hand, the face (of God), His coming down in the canopies of clouds, His coming, going, laughter, shame, anger are all correct (in linguistic use), only the way of their use and their context show whether they have been employed metaphorically or literally". Now, in the passages which these commentators bring to show the metaphorical use of phrases, this may be admitted, for these passages do not mislead anyone as to their meaning. But as for the saying of God the Exalted "(Do they then await that God should come) in the canopies of clouds"?[47] and, again, His saying "Do they (i.e. the infidels) then await that angels should come to them, or that the Lord or some of His signs should come to them?"[48]—with regard to these, the use of metaphor or allegory—to employ these categories (of the commentators)—cannot even be imagined. If God intended to use iḍmār[49] in these sayings, then He has been happy and content to mislead (people) and cast them in error.

'But as for the saying of God the Exalted "God's hand is upon theirs",[50] and ('Woe betide me for) having fallen short (in my duty) to God (literally to the side of God)',[51] these do admit of latitude for metaphorical expression and no two persons versed in the art of Arabic rhetoric dispute this, and the meaning of these verses is quite clear to those who know Arabic well, contrary to the verses quoted earlier. Indeed, just as these verses leave no doubt that they are metaphorical, similarly those others leave no doubt that they are not metaphors but are intended to be taken literally.

'But let us grant that all these are metaphors. Where, then, we ask, are the texts which give a clear indication of pure Unity to which doubtlessly the essence of this righteous Faith—whose greatness is acclaimed by the wise men of the entire world—invites? . . .

(p. 49, 15) 'Upon my life, if God the Exalted did charge a prophet that he should communicate the reality about these (theological) matters to the masses with dull natures and with their minds tied down to pure sensibles, and then constrained him to pursue relentlessly and successfully the task of bringing faith and salvation to the multitude, and then, to crown all, charge him to undertake the purificative training of all the souls so that they may be able to understand these truths, then He has certainly laid upon him a duty incapable of fulfilment by any man—unless the ordinary man receives a special gift from God, a supernal power or a divine inspiration, in which case the instrumentality of the prophet will be superfluous.

'But let us even grant that the Arabian Revelation is metaphor and allegory according to the usage of the Arabic language (which the commentators claim for it). What will they say about the Hebrew Revelation—a monument of utter anthropomorphism from the beginning to the end? One cannot say that that Book is tempered with through and through, for how can this be the case with a book disseminated through innumerable peoples living in distant lands, with so different ambitions—like Jews and Christians with all their mutual antagonisms?

'All this shows that religions are intended to address the multitude in terms intelligible to them, seeking to bring home to them what transcends their intelligence by means of metaphor and symbol. Otherwise, religions would be of no use whatever.'

Immediately follows Avicenna's challenge to the orthodoxy, 'How can then the external form of religion be adduced as an argument in these matters? For if we suppose (as, indeed, I do) that the phenomena of the hereafter are spiritual, not physical and that their truth is inaccessible to the common intelligence, even then the only way open to the religions in their task of inviting people to and warning them of these matters is not clear (philosophical) proof but mere symbolism which may bring these nearer to their understanding. How then can one thing (i.e. the materialistic symbols of religion) be manipulated as a proof for another (i.e. the purely spiritual character of the after-life) for even if this latter were not what we suppose it to be (i.e. even if the after-life were not spiritual or purely spiritual), even then the former would remain as they are (i.e. would remain as material symbols; only, in this case they would not be mere symbols but literal truth).

'After all this discourse let me put to him who will be one of the elect and not amongst the multitude: is the external form of religion usable as an argument in these matters?'

This somewhat long and extreme statement on the value of

Revelation as an index to reality seems to me to contradict clearly what Avicenna usually says elsewhere (see e.g. the quotation from the *Najāt* in n. 39). Further, his unwillingness to avail himself of the non-materialistic passages of the revealed texts—which he here dismisses as being very general and even as being not literally true (for these put the whole emphasis on the absolute transcendence of God) and on which Philo had based *his* allegorization—seems to me to deprive him of all means to interpret the Koran by the Koran itself. All this is done in order to keep a sharp cleavage between the intellectual oligarchy and the multitude of the stupid—again a Greek legacy of which we shall speak more in the last section of this chapter and trace its consequences in the third chapter.

III *Miracles, Prayer, Theurgy*

Avicenna's doctrine of miracles, magic and prayer is based on a new interpretation of the Stoic–neo-Platonic doctrine of Sympathy, and he allows for the effects of these three only in so far as this naturalizing religious concept of Hellenism would carry him. Not all kinds of miracles are, therefore, possible for him for certain events are 'evidently impossible'.[52]

For the Stoics, Sympathy was primarily a 'natural', indeed a physical concept by which they explained, and also which they explained by, their doctrine that the universe is an organic whole of which all the parts behave as members of a single organism. The evidence which they brought to prove this thesis was physical, e.g. the co-variations in the ebb and flow of sea-tides corresponding to the variations in the waning and vexing of the moon etc.[53] In general, they divided the possible relationship of bodies to one another into being (1) united or (2) contiguous or (3) discrete, and concluded that the structure of the body of the universe is of the first kind. Thanks to this union, Sympathy existed in all parts of the structure.

We said in the first section of this chapter[54] that the Stoics believed in a rigorous causal determinism. The concepts, however, of Love, Agreement and Sympathy,[55] by which the Stoics describe the order of the universe, make their world-view essentially very different from that of modern materialistic determinisms. Things in their universe were not purely mechanically moved but sympathetically, and in a living organism, as they believed the world to be, occurrences are possible which are no longer possible in a mechanically determined universe. Indeed, as we said above,[56] the Stoics explained not only the physical phenomena but also those of prophecy, by their principle of Sympathy. Lastly, the Stoics emphasized the influence of the heavenly bodies on earthly events.[57]

Plotinus, in whose thinking super-naturalism and astrology are very influential factors, took over the doctrine of Sympathy from the Stoics and put an extreme interpretation upon it. Since he was not interested in physical sciences, mechanical causation means to him but little for which he *substitutes* Sympathy and 'action at a distance',[58] or rather, since, one soul, according to him, pervades the entire universe, the purely physical categories of 'contiguous action' and 'action at a distance' evaporate. Plotinus also uses the concept of magic as being co-extensive with that of Sympathy and he explains the former by the latter. Sympathy works on the bodily nature and the irrational emotions but not on rational contemplation and will,[59] so does magic. The model of all magic is the Primary Magician, the Eros, which attracts every lover to its beloved. Indeed, Plotinus regards every situation magical (i.e. 'sympathetic') where one thing is related to another.[60] Finally, the influence of prayer, which is a form of magic, must be explained on the basis of Sympathy, since prayer, when addressed to the heavenly bodies, draws their response by a sympathetic necessity and not by their conscious will.[61]

All these Stoic–neo-Platonic tenets of Sympathy constitute the basis of Avicenna's doctrine of revelation, prayer and miracles. Indeed, just as prophetic revelation—as we saw before—is the cognitive aspect of the working of Sympathy, so the efficacy of prayers and the performance of miracles is its practical aspect. Although we are not directly concerned here with the question of prayer, it may be briefly pointed out that for Avicenna, the manner in which miracles are worked by prophets and saints and that in which ordinary people successfully operate through prayer are essentially similar, the only difference is that of degree. Specially relevant to the theme of prayer are his three small treatises published by F. Mehren, *Traités Mystiques d'Avicenne* (Vol. III). In the *Treatise on Love*, Avicenna describes the bond of Cosmic Love by which all things in the universe hang together and on account of which especially every lower being yearns for its superior from which certain potencies peculiar to it emanate into the former. This Cosmic Sympathy is then employed in the *Treatise Concerning the*

Visitation of Shrines to explain the benefits which accrue from pilgrimage. When several bodies meet together, we are told, in the proximity of the body of a saint (or a prophet) or, generally speaking, in a sacred place, they become powerful in sympathetically moving the forces of the Supernal Realm. In this work, Avicenna says that this physical communion in pilgrimages results not only in purely material but also spiritual benefits for the pilgrims. In his third treatise, *On Prayer*, however, he distinguishes, following Plotinus[62] and Porphyry,[63] between an inner spiritual prayer and the outer physical ritual, e.g. ablutions, chanting certain formulae, making certain bodily movements. What, he asks, can be the benefit of the latter? And he answers that thereby the human body receives from the heavenly bodies or the Active Intellect certain influences whereby it is conserved and kept in health, or, in other words, the body and physical life try, in this way, to assimilate themselves to the heavenly bodies in so far as their nature allows them to do so.[64]

It should be pointed out at this stage that although Avicenna accepts a kind of theurgic magic in connection with the ritualistic part of prayer and also in connection with certain occult and obscure happenings both in the souls of men and in nature, his general tendency is to avoid the extravagant mystery-mongering of later Hellenistic magic and theurgy for which he substitutes as naturalizing and sober explanations as possible. The so-called theurgic rituals by which the ancients claimed to charm and even bind their gods in order to achieve revelation and prophecy, he explains, not by saying that such procedures influence the Divine but the human soul itself.[65] And he clearly states that miracles and magical feats are accomplished by the power of the mind itself which is capable of directly affecting matter, not through any magical materials, thus seeking to restrict the domain of the occult. In the *Ishārāt* (III, pp. 254–55) he says:—

'Strange occurrences which take place in the natural world are due to three causes (1) the (powerful) quality of the soul mentioned before (2) natural properties of the elemental bodies like the attraction of iron by magnet due to the latter's peculiar power (3) influences of the heavenly bodies on certain earthly bodies which have certain definite relations of situation with the former, and on certain minds, which are endowed with certain peculiar active and passive states and qualities, these influences being due to similarities existing between the heavenly bodies and earthly existents. The first group is that of magic and miracles, the second of natural wonders (nairanj), the third of talismans.'

This interp·etation of the doctrine of Sympathy, which substitutes the soul itself for the theurgic magic of later Hellenism, is based on the essential divinity of the human soul. This is what guarantees the influence of the soul on the body and on matter in general.[66] Avicenna, who has spoken on the subject frequently, has described this influence at different levels. The soul is a substance which organizes its own body, preserves and controls it:

'It is because of the domination of the soul on its body that the vegetative faculty becomes either weak or strong when the soul becomes conscious of certain judgments which it likes or dislikes— both this like and dislike not being physical at all. This happens when a judgment takes place in the soul: the judgment does not influence the body as a pure belief but rather when this belief is followed by an affection of joy or grief.[67] Now, joy and grief too are something perceived by the soul and do not affect the body as such but influence the vegetative faculty. Thus joy, which is an occurrence in the rational soul, intensifies the action of the vegetative faculty, while the opposite affection of grief, which also occurs in the rational soul and is not a bodily pain, weakens and destroys the action of the vegetative faculty—indeed it can sometimes shatter the very temperament of the body.' (_Shifā'_, _Psychology_, I, 3).

The most common form of the influences of the soul on the body is in the sphere of voluntary movement of the body which Avicenna describes in Aristotelian terms at the beginning of (_Shifā'_ _Psychology_, IV, 4); when one wishes or wills to move the body in a certain direction or towards a certain object, the bodily faculties, if in sound health, obey forthwith. The metaphysical explanation of this ordinary phenomenon too must rest on the subsequently formulated principle that it is of the nature of matter to obey the higher principle, the mind.[68]

From this most common mode of voluntary movement, Avicenna passes on to the influence of the unreflecting emotions, a subject which seems to have interested Greek philosophers, more especially perhaps the Platonizing Stoic, Poseidonious [69] and his successors. We have already noticed in the last section the power of suggestion exercised by imagination whereby emotions are stirred up and bodily members moved:

'We do not regard it impossible that something should occur to the soul in so far as it is in the body and is then followed by affections peculiar to the body itself. Imagination, too, in as much as it is knowledge, is not in itself a bodily affection, but it may happen that as its result certain bodily (i.e. sexual) organs should expand. This is not through any physical cause which necessitates a change in the temperament . . . and so causes the expansion of the organ. Indeed, when a form (i.e. idea) obtains in the imagination, it necessitates a change in the temperament resulting in heat, humidity and air, which, but for that (mental) form, there is nothing to produce.'[70]

Avicenna goes on: 'We say that on the whole it is of the nature of the soul that through it changes occur in the temperament of the bodily matter whithout any bodily action or affection. Thus heat and cold are produced without there being a hot or cold body. To be sure, when an image becomes strong and firm in the soul, the bodily matter is not slow to accept a corresponding form or quality.

'This is because the substance of the soul is (derived from) certain (higher) principles (i.e. Active Intellects) which clothe matter with forms contained in them, such that these forms actually constitute matter. . . . If these principles can bestow upon matter forms constitutive of natural species . . . it is not improbable that they can also bestow qualities, without there being any need of physical contact, action or affection. . . . The form existing in the soul is the cause of what occurs in matter. The form of health existing in a doctor's mind, produces cure and the form of chair existing in a carpenter's mind (produces an actual chair), but such forms cannot translate themselves into actuality except by means of tools and other media: they need these instruments because of their weakness and (relative) inefficacy'.[71]

Next, Avicenna gives a medical example from abnormal psychology: 'Consider the case of a really sick man who firmly believes he has become well and of a (physically) healthy man who is obsessed by the idea that he is ill. It often happens that in such cases, when the idea becomes firmly fixed in the imagination, the bodily matter is accordingly affected and health or illness ensue. Indeed, in such cases, the efficacy of imagination is greater than any doctor could achieve by instruments and media.' 'This is the reason,' he goes on, 'that a man can run fast on a plank of wood when it is put across a well-trodden path, but when it is put like a bridge over a chasm, he would hardly be able to creep over it. This is because he pictures to himself a (possible) fall so vividly that the natural power of his limbs accords with it. . . .'[72]

After depicting the influence of the soul on its own body by pointing to ordinary emotional experiences and medical evidence, Avicenna announces the possibility of miracles: 'When, therefore, ideas and beliefs in them become firmly fixed in the soul, they necessarily come to exist in actuality. . . . In the case of the Universal Soul, these ideas may influence the entire Nature, while in the case of individual souls, they may affect a particular part of Nature. (So), often a soul can influence other bodies like its own body as in the case of the evil eye and "suggestion by concentration of imagination (al-wahm al-'āmil)". Indeed, when a soul is powerful and noble, resembling the higher principles, matter throughout the world obeys it, is affected by it and actually receives forms which exist in such a soul. This is because, as we shall show later, the human soul (unlike the animal soul) is not imprinted in the body but is related to it only in so far as it cares for it and controls it. If this kind of relationship gives the soul the possibility to change the bodily matter from what its nature requires, it is nothing wonderful that a powerful and noble[73] soul should exert its influence beyond its own body, if it is not deeply immersed in its inclination to this body and has at the same time both a dominating nature and powerful *habitus* (acquired through practice).'

Our philosopher, however, tells us, while speaking of the soul-body relationship in general (*Shifā'*, *Psychology*, V, 3): 'The originated body is the soul's kingdom and instrument, and in the substance of the soul which originates simultaneously with the body —a body whose existence has called forth the soul's origination from the primary principles—there is a natural impulse to occupy itself with the body, to use it, to care for it and to be attracted towards it. These conditions become peculiar to the soul and turn it away from all other bodies', and the corresponding passage of the Najāt adds 'except through its own'. In the case of ordinary human beings, then, the direct influence of the soul is restricted to its own body, while the exceptional souls of the prophets and the saints,[74] by becoming 'World souls, as it were',[75] become operative throughout Nature. They can 'cure the sick and make evil persons sick, disintegrate and integrate organisms . . . and by their will ruins and prosperity, the sinking of the earth and plagues occur.'[76] This practical aspect is in fact, parallel to the cognitive aspect: just as the prophetic revelation is *ab initio* independent of the body and sense-perception, whereas ordinary cognition is necessarily conditioned by them, similarly, in action, the prophetic soul is independent of its body.

Despite his insistence on the virtuosity of the miracle-working soul, Avicenna affirms the reality of black magic, although he adds that the black magician ultimately loses the power of his soul: 'When a man possesses this (psychic power of influencing other bodies) but is evil and mis-employs it in working mischief, he is an evil magician. By his excessive indulgence in this, the powerful quality of his soul disintegrates (gradually) and he has no influence where there are sages.'[77] (*Ishārāt*, III, p. 254).

Although Avicenna's account of miracles (as well as that of prophetic inspiration) is, for the most part, founded upon more refined spiritual-psychological basis than the cruder theurgy of later Hellenism, encumbered by mythology and superstition, there are, nevertheless, two serious modifications. The first of these we have encountered above where Avicenna speaks of the talismanic occurrences due to occult astrological influences. The second is the role of good and evil demons in producing miraculous events, although, as appears from the following, these demonic souls are not supernatural powers but the irrational souls of departed human beings.

Describing the opinion of some philosophers,[78] Avicenna says (*R. Aḍḥawiya*, pp. 123, 12–24, 10): 'The imaginative faculty can be separated from matter (at death) through the rational faculty. Such a soul can then contemplate all the images existing in the entire sensible nature (but not the purely intelligible ideas) since the whole of the sensible world becomes its body, as it were, in which it becomes imprisoned, not being able to rise higher to the spiritual realm. It can then know all the particular causes in the world—since none of these is entitled to be more known than the others—and so fore-knows the events resulting from particular movements (of the stars). In this way the (lower) bodily soul, with which it is in contact, also comes to have a fore-knowledge of future events.

'These philosophers say the evil souls among these are then

more powerful to do evil, since, being rid of their particular body which restricted their movements, the whole material realm becomes uniformly their field of action, and similarly, good souls are able to do more good. These people unanimously call the evil souls demons (devils) and the good ones of this imperfect (since they are irrational) class of souls, the jinn. They also posit for the jinn and for the devils a contact with men and certain spiritual actions from which certain (occult) natural occurrences result.'

The contact of such departed souls with living people is described in the previous section of the same work (p. 123). The deceased soul cannot inhere in a living body because the transmigration of souls has been shown to be impossible on other grounds (following Aristotle). The demonic soul, therefore, makes a spiritual contact with a living person and influences his character, aspirations etc. whereby wicked persons can become more potently wicked and good men more potently good.[79]

IV *The Mission and the Law (Da'wa and Sharī'a)*

It is an integral function of the prophet's office that he, as we have already seen in the Second Section, should come forth to his people or to humanity at large with a religio-social mission and should legislate. The prophet is, thus, not a mere 'thinker' or a 'mystic', but an actor moulding actual history on a definite pattern. Before we describe the Muslim philosophers' doctrine on this subject and trace historically the ideas which make it up, it should be remarked at the outset—and we shall revert to this later—that this aspect of the philosophical doctrine of prophecy comes nearest to expressing the *esprit* of the historic Muslim community.

Avicenna's account of the genesis of the moral order in the society is based on the conception of a kind of 'social contract' as a dire necessity to control the aggressive excesses of self-interest and provide a *modus vivendi*. This type of morality exists, and must exist, for the masses; it is only a few good men who can transcend the conflict of individual interests and for whom the Law is not merely a *pis aller* but a preparation for true spiritual elevation and bliss:

'It is clear that man differs from other animals in that if he were alone, managing all his affairs by himself without someone else's co-operation in fulfilling his needs, his life will not be elegant. It is therefore essential that human life be based on co-operation. . . . And, for this reason, people have been forced to establish cities and contract societies. Those who are unwise enough not to establish cities with laws but are content to have a mere gregarious life, without legal and contractual bases, only remotely resemble men . . . . This being clear, it is necessary for man to live by co-operation; co-operation entails contracts and transactions . . . which themselves are impossible without law and justice. Law and justice are impossible without a law-giver and a determinator of justice.

'Now, such a being must be a man for he must be capable of addressing people and enforcing law. He cannot leave people to argue among themselves so that every one of them may regard his own self-interest as justice and the opposite as injustice. . . .'[80]

After these introductory remarks, I propose to describe the philosophers' theory in order to elicit some sort of answer to the following questions:—

(1) Why is a *prophet* needed for the foundation of the law? Or, why has the law to have a religious basis?
(2) Why *must* the prophet be a law-giver?
(3) What is the criterion for recognizing a true law-giver?
(4) What is the relation of the moral-legal values to truth-values?

This brief outline would then, it is hoped, enable us to determine to what extent, if any, the Muslim philosophers were influenced by traditional Islam and effected, or attempted to effect, an adjustment between it and their philosophy.

The law, as the above quotation has indicated, must be founded by a prophet. This is because the function of law is to check the excessive self-interests of people and pedagogically to lead them, or the more gifted among them, to the real intention of the law-giver which is a vision of the higher truth. It is, therefore, essential for the law-giver that he himself be in possession of the religio-philosophical truth and, further, that he be capable of expressing himself in legal and formal terms and doctrines which can negotiate and are acceptable to the common intelligence. Now, as has been shown previously, only a prophet by the acuteness of his intellect, and the power of his imagination, is able to achieve this:

'It is obvious that when the intelligibles concerning voluntary actions, which it is the function of the practical philosophy to yield, are actually formulated, they must be accompanied by certain conditions through which alone they can become actual. . . . Thus, the law-giver is a man who has the power to deduce, through the excellence of his cogitation, the conditions through which these practical intelligibles can be actually realized for the attainment of ultimate Happiness. . . . Now, it is not possible to deduce these conditions . . . and, indeed, it is not possible even to conceive the practical intelligibles by which the law-giver occupies the position of the First Ruler, unless he has previously possessed philosophy (through his contact with the Active Intelligence).'[81]

Further, the law must be such that it continues to be accepted by people after the law-giver's death. Indeed, this is why law is necessary, for if prophets frequented this world, their authority being greater than that of the law, the latter could be suitably altered and adjusted according to the needs of the time: 'Just as the founder of a religious law can alter his own law if he thinks this more suitable at a later date, similarly a succeeding law-giver can alter his predecessor's law, for if this predecessor were alive at this later date he himself would have changed it. At times, however, when such a law-giver is not present, the laws prescribed by the (earlier) law-giver must be recorded and adopted and the State governed according to them.'[82]

Now, in order that the law continues to be effective after the prophet's death in the sense that the prophet's real intentions and his background meaning is not forgotten and so the law not reduced to a moribund formalism, it is necessary that the law-giver establish certain definite religious institutions, serving as constant reminders of the real purpose of the law—and this only a prophet, a recipient of religious revelation—thanks to his strong imaginative faculty— can do:

'Now such a man who is a prophet, does not recur at all times for matter recipient of such a perfection rarely constitutes such a temperament. It is thus necessary that the prophet establish certain (religious) institutions for the perpetuation of the law he has promulgated for human welfare. Undoubtedly, the benefits of this are the perpetuation of people in their continued knowledge of the Maker and of the hereafter and the removal of the causes of forgetfulness (on their part) after the end of the generation immediately succeeding the prophet. It is therefore necessary that the prophet should institute certain acts which he makes incumbent upon people to perform constantly . . . so that they should remind them afresh (of the purpose of the law). . . . These acts must be such as keep in people's hearts the memory of God the Exalted and of the hereafter, else they would be useless. Now, "reminders" can be either words uttered or intentions made in one's mind. It should be said to people, "these actions would bring you near unto God and would cause the blessed good to come to you"—and indeed, they should be really such. These are like the several forms of worship made incumbent upon people.'[83]

We shall now try to give a historical analysis of the ideas contained in the above answer to our first question. So far as the quotations from al-Fārābī are concerned, if we leave out their identification of the law-giver with the prophet, they are purely Platonic. That ideally the law-giver or the king must be a philosopher is too famous a Platonic doctrine to need documentation. That of the two–the law and the law-giver–the more important factor is the law-giver who, if need be, can and must change the law, but that the formulation of the law is, nevertheless, necessary since the true law-giver is a rarity, is Plato's teaching in the *Politicus*:

297 (B): 'That no great number of men . . . could ever acquire the kingly science and be able to administer a state with wisdom, but our one right form of government must be sought in some small number or one person, and all other forms are, merely, as we said before, more or less successful imitations of that. . . .

(D) 'Tell me this: Assuming that the form of government we have described is the only right form, do you not see that the *other forms* (i.e. where there is no philosopher-king) must employ its written laws if they are to be preserved. . . .' The philosopher-king (and he alone) may and indeed must change laws. (ibid 295 B): 'Let us suppose that a physician or a gymnastic trainer is going away and expects to be a long time absent from his patients or pupils; if he thinks they will not remember his instructions, would he not want to write them down? . . .

'But what if he should come back again after a briefer absence than he expected? Would he not venture to substitute other rules for those written instructions if others happened to be better for his patients, because the winds or something else had, by act of God, changed unexpectedly from their usual course? . . .'

There is, however, nothing specifically religious about the Platonic conception of the philosopher-king in the sense that he is not identified with a person in whom a special divine faculty, like some form of revelation, inheres. For this we have to turn to the cults of heroes and kings in remote antiquity and their subsequent rationalizations by philosophers and 'socio-cultural historians', as we indicated above.[84] The ancient mythology contained in its pantheon, which was the object of popular honour and worship, heroes and gods of all kinds—war-leaders, kings, statesmen, and supposed inventors of socio-cultural amenities like agriculture, weaving etc. [85] The belief that in the Golden Age the kings were gods was an integral part of this mythology. With Hekataius, however, began the movement to disentangle 'history' from myth and to interpret the heroes as men who, because of their great services to humanity, had earned honour and veneration.

This 'historiographical' movement, known, after its most famous representative, as Euhemerism, had its philosophical counterpart which, at least in its systematized form, was formulated by the Stoics, and declared such deified benefactors of humanity to be sages: (*Aëtius, Plac.*, I, 6, 9 sq.): 'That is why those who have made traditions about the gods, have represented their worship in three forms, firstly, natural, secondly mythical and thirdly that attested by the law. The natural was taught by the philosophers, the mythical by the poets and the legal by every state.[86] The whole doctrine (of gods) is divided into seven kinds. The first consists of the stars and the atmospheric phenomena. . . . The seventh and the last class comprises those who, although born as men, like Heracles . . . and Dionysus, were nevertheless venerated because of their beneficial deeds for the social life.' Indeed, every kind of greatness and extra-ordinary achievement in the human race was explained on the hypothesis of some divine factor: 'Nemo igitur vir magnus sine aliquo adflatu divino unquam fuit. . . . Magna di curant, parva neglegunt. Magnis autem viris prosperae semper omnes res' (Cicero, *De Natura Deorum*, II, 66). Again, Cicero, ibid, II, 24 'Suscepit autem vita hominum consuetudoque communis ut beneficiis excellentis viros in caelum fama ac voluntate tollerent. Hinc Hercules hinc Castor . . . quorum cum remanerent animi atque aeternitate fruerentur, rite di sunt habiti, cum et optimi essent et aeterni.' In popular mythology Demeter e.g. was celebrated both for her discovery of agriculture and her foundation of the law.

In Muslim eclecticism, however, where prophetic revelation, the intellectual consummation of a philosopher and the poetic art of imaginative creativity were all combined in one ideal personality, it becomes still easier to ground the law in a religious basis of revelation. The motivating force of this eclecticism, as we shall presently see, is, of course, the actual image of the Prophet Muḥammad as it was developed in the mind of the Muslim Community generally. The only thing in this perfectionist picture that itched in this case as it did in Philo's conception of Moses as philosopher was the forced factor of intellectualism.

A real law-giver must, therefore, be a prophet-philosopher. But, conversely, every true prophet-philosopher must be a law-giver. A true prophet or a genuine philosopher, merely by virtue of being this, cannot remain within the confines of his own personality but must go forth to humanity, or to a nation,[87] both with a divinely revealed religion and with a law based upon it. He must be able to formulate his religious consciousness into a definite pattern of religio-political life for people to follow. From this, again, it would be obvious how the ordinary or 'imperfect' mystics and philosophers are to be distinguished from the prophet or the true philosopher.

This point is implied in Avicenna's account of the political aspect of the doctrine of prophecy,[88] but is dealt with more explicitly by al-Fārābī (Taḥṣil-al-Saʿāda, p. 42):

'It is thus necessary that a law-giver, whose essence is that of a Ruler, not of a servant, be a philosopher, and, conversely, in the case of the philosopher who has acquired theoretical virtues, these acquisitions would be worthless if he does not possess the ability to realize them in all other people in so far as this is possible. . . . These cannot be realized in other people, in so far as this is possible, except through an excellent persuasive and imaginative power (i.e. which transform the pure truth of philosophy into persuasive symbols).

'Thus, the meaning of the Imām, of the philosopher and of the law-giver is identical. True, philosophy in itself denotes (only) theoretical excellence; but if this excellence is pursued to its ultimate perfection in all respects, it must embrace the other abilities. Similarly, the concept of law-giver denotes an excellence of the knowledge of deducing the conditions of practical intelligibles and of actualizing them in peoples and states; but if these are to be based on knowledge, they must be preceded by theoretical excellence: they are related to each other as a consequent is related to its antecedent.'[89]

The real and ultimate aim, as has now emerged, of the state and its laws is the diffusion of philosophy among people, *in so far as this is possible*, and bringing them near unto God, or, as Plato has it, it is the 'tendance of the soul'. Even according to Avicenna, who starts by giving an account of the *origin* of morality and law as a dire necessity to prevent excessive self-interest, the *end* of law is to prepare men for a spiritual purpose: 'the benefit of religious acts (conceived not in a narrow sense but as embracing the whole of the Sharī'a) is the perpetuation of the Apostolic Law by which people's existence is secured, and that they are brought near unto God through purification' (*Najāt*, p. 308, 7–9). So al-Fārābī: 'Philosophy of this description (i.e. one which does not remain personal but aims at self-propagation at large, in so far, of course, as is possible) has come to us only from the Greeks—from Plato and Aristotle. Neither of these has given us mere (theoretical) philosophy, without also giving us the ways to it and methods of re-creating it (among men) when it is destroyed or become distorted' (*Taḥṣīl al Sa'āda*, p. 47, 3–5).

It is this kind of doctrine of the inter-dependence of theory and practice which has produced the amalgam of Muḥammad cum Plato-Aristotle. It results in a type of pragmatism which says that true philosophy must be workable in history, and conversely, that that which has successfully worked in history must be true philosophy. It supplements the images both of the prophet of Islam and of the Greek philosophers. Muḥammad was a prophet who not only gave a good but a successful law to the world; surely, he must have been a philosopher? And if Muḥammad was a true philosopher, in promulgating his religion and law he must have but talked only in successful parables down to people. Conversely, since the Greek personalities in question and others were undoubtedly great philosophers and they did not, indeed, keep their philosophy to themselves, but formulated actual theories of state and law on its basis, surely, they were divinely inspired prophets?[90] Only here we have to stop one step short, for these philosophers do not quite come up to the pragmatic criterion of success:

'The real philosopher is such as has been described in these pages. If, even though he is a perfect philosopher, people do not benefit from him, this is not through a fault of his but because of those who do not listen to him and those who do not think it proper that he should be listened to. The king-imām, then, is such by virtue of his essence and his art, irrespective of whether he finds people who would accept him or not, whether he is obeyed or not, whether he finds a people who co-operate with him in realizing his purpose or not, just as a physician is such by his essence and his art and by his ability to treat the sick, irrespective of whether he finds patients or not, can obtain suitable instruments for his work or not, be he poor or rich. But, just as in the case of the physician, it cannot be absolutely established whether he is a real physician or a seeming one, except if some of these factors obtain, similarly, the imamate of an imam, the philosophy of a philosopher and the rulership of a king is never beyond doubt unless he can procure instruments to use in his work and people whose service he can use to the achievement of his ends.'[91] (al-Fārābī, Taḥṣīl al-Saʿāda, pp. 46, 12–47, 2).

Therefore, although the Muslim philosophers affirm the divine missionary character of the leading Greek thinkers, their principle of the successful executability of this mission in actual history, tends to emphasize rather the figures of Moses, Jesus and, *par excellence*, of Muḥammad. That is why the philosophical image of the Prophet has much more grafted on it than the images of the Greek thinkers (who are represented more or less faithfully according to the late Hellenic tradition), for the formal Greek characteristics of a primarily intellectual perfection are required as a base for the understanding and interpretation of an *actual historical paradigm*. It may be said that the subject-matter of this doctrine is the personality of Muḥammad, the formal characteristics Hellenic. This may sound a platitude, but it is an important one, for it shows that in framing this image the philosophers acted from a genuine and sincere motive and were not merely artificially trying to engraft

Greek doctrines on Islam. Nor is it necessary, I think, that the Muslim philosophers should have derived their principle of success entirely from the history of Islam itself. The principle is assumed in the ancient cults of rulers where religion and politics went hand in hand—the divine must succeed and the successful must be divine. The Iranian-Hellenic doctrines of the Tyche in this connection are an intellectual expression of this assumption. It was, therefore, both natural and easy for the philosophers to engraft the invisible to the visible—a philosophical back-ground to an actually successful religio-political order—than vice-versa.

But let us now examine the philosophers' conception of the relation of law to philosophy. Religious law, is, of course, based on the inculcation of certain beliefs about God, the world and after-life. Now these beliefs, as shown above in Section II of this chapter, are, according to our philosophers, not beliefs in pure truth but in symbols of that truth. Correspondingly, the law which is but a method of realizing these beliefs—beliefs which may serve as pedagogy for the finer members of the community and lead them on to higher truth but which must remain literal truth for the bulk —must in itself remain a lower discipline than the study of philosophy itself. In Section II we have given Avicenna's and al-Fārābī's statements on their conception of the relationship between philosophy and religion or, rather, between 'philosophic religion' and 'organized religions'. Here is a very graphic picture of how the philosopher is to realize both theoretical and practical philosophy in society. After saying that a perfect philosopher is only he who can devise a method of actualizing philosophical truth, al-Fārābī says (*Taḥṣīl al-Saʿāda* p. 40, 5 sq.).

'To make others understand something is of two kinds: either by making its essence to be truly conceived or communicating an image which symbolizes it. Similarly, judgment is formed in two ways: either by a convincing rational argument or by persuasion.[92] When (immaterial) existents are known and conceived in their essences and judgments are formed of them on convincing rational arguments, this knowledge constitutes philosophy, but when imagination receives their imitative symbols and judgments are formed about these symbols by the persuasive method, this type of knowledge was termed by the ancients "religion".[93] When, however, the truth itself is sought to communicate by persuasive means (rather than rational), the religion thus generated is called "the commonplace mutilated philosophy."[94]

'Religion, thus according to them, symbolizes philosophy although they are both concerned with the very same objects and both seek to give the ultimate principles of existence, for they give the First Principle and Cause, the ultimate purpose of man—which constitutes his ultimate Happiness—and of each other existent. (The only difference is that) whatever philosophy gives as a rational concept, religion gives as an image and wherever philosophy demonstrates by argument, religion merely persuades.

'Thus, whereas philosophy gives the essence of the First Principle and of the immaterial secondary principles . . . in a rational form, religion figurizes them by images taken from material principles and *principles of state. Similarly, it figurizes the divine acts by the acts of the principles of state, the acts of natural forces and principles, by suitable volitional faculties, habits and arts*, as Plato does in the *Timaeus*. Religion's figurization of the rationals by sensibles is e.g. the representation of matter by Hell or Darkness or Water,[95] or of non-existence by Darkness. In the same way, the types of ultimate happiness which are the ends of human virtuous activity are symbolized by goods which are only seemingly happiness, [96] . . . the several grades of (eternal) existence are symbolized by the ranks of temporal existence.[97] In all this, the symbols should be as near to reality as possible. . . . Philosophy is temporally prior to religion.'

Whence comes the doctrine that a Milla—a legally instituted religious community or the religious ideals of a group together with the state-laws as the machinery for realizing them—is an 'imitation' philosophy, never capable of rising to the higher truth, but an inevitable instrument of making people relatively good? The idea that the state and the law are of a lower order than philosophy and only approximations to it, is affirmed by Plato in the latter part of the *Politicus*, but that, according to him, is the case only when the ideal law-giver is not actually present. That inherently and under all conditions, statecraft must fail to realize the highest goal and is doomed to realize only a 'symbolic' bliss is not a Platonic doctrine. Nor is the doctrine Aristotelian. For, although for Aristotle, the life of contemplation is better than that of action, he nowhere conceives of the state as existing purely or primarily for the masses who are eternally doomed to a shadow-happiness.

The solution of the problem lies in the Stoic conception of the 'tripartite theology' according to which the 'civil' theology or religion, as opposed to the philosophic religion, is the lot of the masses who can not only not understand philosophy but *must* not understand it for it would harm their religion. This doctrine was formulated by the Stoic Panätius as a defence of the popular religion against the onslaught of the Hellenic enlightenment. The pagan Roman pontiff, Scaevola gave it clerical authority.[98]

It is to be noted that in Islamic philosophy there is, strictly speaking, nothing which corresponds to the 'mythical' or 'poetical' division of theology. The reason is that the Greeks had no revealed scripture as such but Homer and Hesiod had, during the centuries, deeply influenced the religious life of the people and were later regarded by the Stoics as sages. In this process, poetry itself had come to be regarded as something quasi-divine, giving a peep, even though a blinking one, into reality. But the poets had, at the same time, conjured up extraordinary crude and silly pictures of the gods and the after-life. It therefore became imperative for the Stoics to distinguish this kind of theology from the philosophical and the civil. But even so the philosopher Varro, according to whom the 'poetical' theology is meant for the theatre, the 'natural' for the philosopher and the 'civil' for the state-community,[99] admits that the last one partakes of the other two, especially the poetical:

'Ait enim (Varro), ea quae scribunt poetae, minus esse quam ut populi sequi debeant; quae autem philosophi, plus quam ut ea vulgum scrutari expediat. "Quae sic abhorrent", inquit, "ut tamen ex utroque genere ad civiles rationes assumpta sint non pauca. . . ."' (Augustine, op. cit. VI, 6). It thus turns out that 'civil theology' or positive religion embodies in its laws certain poetic images or symbols with some mixture of pure or philosophical theology.

Now, this exactly seems to correspond to the Muslim philosophers' conception of the Milla. The Milla contains certain hints about the pure truth but is essentially constituted by symbols, although these symbols are the best since they are the absolute minimum for the common man and avoid the extravagance of the 'artistic' religion. We see therefore that the essential theory is the same although its terms have substantially changed. No doubt, this fact makes it easier, not more difficult, for the philosophers to defend Islam with the help of this scheme, than it had been for a pagan Scaevola to defend *his* popular religion.

Nor, indeed do the Muslim philosophers envisage that the philosopher can remain above or beyond the Milla: 'A philosopher must perform the external (bodily) acts and observe the duties of the law, for if a person disregards a law ordained as incumbent by a prophet and then pursues philosophy, he must be deserted. He should consider unlawful for himself what is unlawful in his Milla.'[100] This is because an ordinary philosopher may *understand* the intentions of the prophet but he cannot institute a new law: 'This (prophetic) status is that of a *teacher* (of the whole Milla) and cannot be reached by every one. My master Aristotle reported his master Plato as saying that the peak of knowledge (gnosis) is too high for any and every bird to reach.'[101]

This is an outline of the historical sources of this doctrine. But why was it adopted? Indeed, the question may be broadened: Why was this fusion of the Peripatetic doctrine of the Intellect, the later neo-Platonic doctrine of the Law of Symbolization, the Stoic doctrine of the inner inspiration and of external para-perceptual experience, and the equally Stoic doctrine of the 'Civil theology' instituted by the sage–Law-giver, carried out to construct a comprehensive and complex theory of prophecy for which there is no parallel in pre-Islamic philosophy, even though each of its several constituents is pre-Islamic? The answer is inevitably that this was done purposely with a view to giving an adequate picture of the Prophet and his actual performance and the doctrine of Intellect was introduced to serve as the necessary base without which the whole superstructure would collapse. There is conclusive evidence that during the medieval Islamic enlightenment, the Sharī'a with its beliefs and laws was in an acute crisis. The first phase of this crisis resolved by al-Ash'ari had barely passed when the philosophical crisis began. The appearance of the famous medical doctor and philosopher Rāzī, who dubbed all positive religions as impostures, was not and cannot have been an isolated incident. Avicenna himself tells us in the preface to his epistle on Prophecy (ap. *Tis' Rasā'il*) of the 'doubts' of his correspondent regarding the Faith, and he has rebuked in more than one place the 'irreligious so-called philosophers', just as he has rebuked the 'common herd' and its leaders. This crisis is similar to that of the Hellenistic paganism which the Stoics tried to avert. But quite apart from this crisis, the philosophers too had a desperate need for understanding Islam themselves in terms of their rationalism.

From this point of view, and within these terms of reference, therefore, the philosophers are justifiably called 'defenders of the Faith'.[102] Their attempt to formulate the theory of revelation was quite conscious and deliberate. Nevertheless, I find it irreconcilable with facts when P. L. Gardet wishes to see in this attempt an 'extension' of the philosophic system on the part of the philosophers (or, at any rate, of Avicenna). Indeed, P. Gardet says [103] that Avicenna has *added* the theory of prophecy, inspired wholly by the Islamic tradition, as something entirely new to the Greek tradition of philosophy. If Islam could bring such far-reaching changes in Avicenna's system, why should he have denied the temporal creation of the World or philosophically rejected the resurrection of the flesh? I find, on the contrary, that every stitch of this elaborate theory has its source in Greek ideas, although many of these ideas, —e.g. the more spiritual and refined idea of sympathy—appear in a less occult and more scientific form. And the intricate eclectic elaboration is, of course, new.

There is much in this theory which, as we shall see, was accepted by the orthodoxy. On the whole, the intellectualist basis of this system, even though foreign to early Islam, was not rejected off-hand, although attempts were made to 'de-naturalize' it as much as possible and in varying degrees. Nor would the orthodox thinkers quarrel with the philosophical view that the anthropomorphic expressions in the Koran about God are not meant to be taken literally.[104] But it is on the positive side as to what they *do mean* that the orthodox violently disagree with the philosophers and tend to place their reliance chiefly on the metaphorical use of the language rather than on allegorization. But the basic trouble was the philosophical conception of the religion—both its beliefs and its laws—as mere symbols from which there is no escape to reality for the masses. Not only did this symbol-reality dichotomy cut at the roots of the traditional Islam: it sought to introduce a distinction of the naturally privileged and the naturally barred in a society to which essential egalitarianism was a cardinal article of faith. The philosophical distinction, in fact, was incurable and far more ominous than the mystic distinction between those having an inner spiritual life and those who were content only with the external observances of the law, for, a para-mystical distinction—that of Islam and Īmān— was accepted by orthodoxy, as expressing a distinction *within a whole*, between the spirit and the letter of the law, and not an absolute separation and disengagement of the two.

NOTES

1. This doctrine also occurs in a treatise called *al-Ta'līqāt* (Haydarabad, 1346 A.H., p. 24, 10 sq.) attributed to al-Fārābī: 'our knowledge is of two kinds: one multiple, which is called the psychic knowledge, and the other non-multiple which is called noetic and simple. For example, if an intelligent ('āqil) man is holding a discussion with a friend who makes a lengthy discourse (i.e. by way of question), the former presents that whole discourse to his mind and, while thus reflecting upon it, he has a certainty (I read yatayaqqanu for yata'ayyanu) that he is going to (i.e. can) answer it without (yet) having any detailed knowledge of the answers (to be given). Then he begins to . . . etc.' It is, however, noteworthy that this treatise embodies also certain other doctrines which contradict al-Fārābī's position outlined in the previous chapter: e.g. it is here maintained that even the potential intellect survives (p. 1, 18) and that the potential intellect is a separate substance (p. 10, 16; p. 12, 15; p. 13, 10). There is also another important consideration concerning the cognitive powers of the heavenly bodies. Al-Fārābī holds that the heavenly bodies have no imagination proper but only intellect and, further, that their intellect has no potentiality whatever (e.g. *Siyāsāt*, p. 5). According to Avicenna, on the other hand, these beings have, in a certain sense, a potential intellect since they possess a discursive, psychic reasoning and further, they have imagination. On this latter doctrine among other things, as we shall see later in this chapter, Avicenna bases his theory of the 'imaginative' prophecy, and on this score, was rebuked by Averroes who in his *Tahāfut al-Tahāfut* (ed. Bouyges, Beirut, 1930, p. 495, 5 sq.) asserts that this view is the invention of Avicenna. For Avicenna's view see Van den Bergh, *Epitom. d. Metaph. des Averroes.* pp. 117–8. Now both these Avicennian doctrines appear in this treatise (p. 9, 19; p. 98, 12).

2. Plotinus, *Enn.* V, 8, 5, speaks of a Wisdom (σοφία) which is not made up of a mass of propositions and theorems but is one and total which then generates and deploys itself in a multiplicity of propositions: οὐκέτι συντεθεῖσαν ἐκ θεωρημάτων, ἀλλ' ὅλην ἕν τι, οὐ τὴν συγκειμένην ἐκ πολλῶν εἰσ ἕν, ἀλλὰ μᾶλλον ἀναλυομένην εἰσ πλῆθος ἐξ ἑνός. In V, 8, 4, Plotinus says that we do not understand this Wisdom because we imagine that knowledge is a mass made up of discrete theorems and propositions which, he contends, is not the case *even with our ordinary knowledge*, let alone of the higher Wisdom. Plotinus builds this doctrine up on the analogy of the creative reason in Nature which he has discussed in V, 8, 3. He speaks of apparently the same Wisdom in IV, 4, 11–12 where it is called φρόνησις. There again the wisdom of the Sage is built on the analogy of

C

Nature; and Plotinus uses such terms as the seminal and creative reason. He also uses terms like certainty and assurance. These are a testimony of the Stoical influence. (See also Chap. I, n. 32)

3. The Stoics had distinguished between the prophecy by Divine Posession or Inspiration which comes without learning, both at intellectual and imaginative levels (cf. Ps.–Plutarch, *Vit. Poes. Hom.* ii, 212: τὸ ἄτεχνον καὶ ἀδίδακτον [τῆς μαντικῆς]) on the one hand, and divination by means of a rational interpretation of signs on the other; cf. *Cic. De Div.* I 18, 34. Iamblichus, in De Myst. (10, 3–4) rejects other kinds of prophecy except that by Inspiration: μόνη τοίνυν ἡ θεία μαντικὴ συναπτομένη τοῖς θεοῖς . . . καὶ τῶν θείων νοήσεων μετέχουσα (10, 4); see below, n. 10.

4. al-'aql al-munfa'il (the passive intellect which al-Fārābī, however, uses interchangeably with 'aql bi'l-fi'l (the actual intellect) both here and in the *Madīna* (pp. 57, 22–58, 16).

5. i.e. by al-Fārābī himself; cf. the list of his works in al-Qifṭī.

6. *Siyāsāt*, p. 49, 4 sq.

7. According to al-Fārābī the Active Intelligence becomes a quasi-form for the prophet's mind, but he never says that the prophetic intellect becomes the Active Intellect itself. The furthest he goes is to say that at this stage the human mind becomes of the *same order* as the Active Intellect.

8. For this doctrine see my *Avicenna's Psychology*, pp. 35–7, 93 sq; the same account appears in the corresponding parts of the _Shifā'_ and the _Ishārāt_.

9. Aristotle (*Anal. Post.* 1, 54) says that some people, by an inborn sagacity (ἀγχίνοια) are able to guess the middle term in an 'imperceptible time'. With the Stoics (*Stoicorum Veterum Fragmenta* III, 66, 7) this 'sagacity' has become a form of knowledge (ἐπιστήμη) by which the wise man is able to discover the right action 'on the spot'; (cf. also the Stoic doctrine that the non-sage becomes a sage with a coup: Plutarch, *Stoic., Repugn.*, 2 sq.). Plutarch himself conceives of the highest mystical illumination as a sudden occurrence like lightning by which the soul, touching the divine being (the Daimon), becomes possessed of total Reality (*De Is* 77): ἡ δὲ τοῦ νοητοῦ καὶ εἰλικρινοῦς καὶ ἀγίου νόησις ὥσπερ ἀστραπὴ διαλάμψασα τῇ ψυχῇ ἅπαξ ποτὲ θιγεῖν καὶ προσιδεῖν παρέσχε . . . πρὸς τὸ πρῶτον ἐκεῖνο καὶ ἁπλοῦν καὶ ἄϋλον ἐξάλλονται καὶ θιγγόντες ἁπλῶς τῆς περὶ αὐτὸ καθαρᾶς ἀληθείας οἰονό ἐντελετῇ τέλος ἔχειν την φιλοσοφίαν νομίζουσι. Cf. Plato (*Phdr.* 250c): ὁλόκληρα καὶ ἁπλᾶ . . . ἐν αὐγῇ καθαρᾷ.

10. In the note 3 above we saw that the Stoics had divided prophecy into two kinds, one 'natural' or by means of inspiration and inspired dreams, the second by rational conjecture through an interpretation of signs. Since everything in the world is bound by an unalterable sequence of causes and effects (or Fate), if one were capable of discerning them all at one glance, there would be no need of the second kind, but as it is, although in ecstasy a prophet may know some of these causes, no human being can know them all (*Cicero De Div.* I, 126–7): 'easdemque causas verisimile est rerum futurarum cerni ab eis qui aut per furorem eas aut in quiete videant. Praeterea cum fato omnia fiant, . . . si quis mortalis possit esse qui colligationem causarum omnium perspiciat animo, nihil eum profecto fallat. . . . Quod cum nemo facere nisi deus possit, relinquendum est homini, ut signis quibusdam consequentia declarantibus futura praesentiat.' See Avicenna's *Najāt*, p. 302, 21 sq. 'if a man could know all the events in earth and in the heavens and their natures, he would know what happens in the future', and the rejection of the claims of astronomers. Now just such an intuitive discernment of the total Reality is envisaged in the Muslim philosophers' doctrine of prophecy and therefore we see that there is no trace here of sign-interpretation: the prophet comes to grasp the whole Reality. See Plutarch's statement in the last note; also *Corp. Herm.* I, 22: καὶ εὐθὺς τὰ πάντα γνωρίζουσι i.e. the gnostics when the NOUS becomes their helper—Iamblichus, *De Myst.* III, 28, rejects divination by art and 'Sympatheia' as being only imperfect images of the 'Divine Prophecy' which is described as a 'unitary reason and order, a single (total and simple) intelligible and immutable truth', incapable of increase or decrease. According to Iamblichus, however, this 'Divine Prophecy' depends entirely on God and is something miraculous, having no ground whatsoever in a natural capacity of the soul. In III, 17 he says that God can bestow wisdom and intelligence on the foolish, a wisdom which excels all knowledge.

For the doctrine that although the NOUS is a unity, it has an order and non-temporal sequence cf. the above quotation from Cicero and Iamblichus; see also *Philo, De Opif. Mundi,* 15–20, Plotinus, *Enn,* III, 8, etc.; cf. also Bergson's doctrine of 'Pure Duration' according to which we are intuitively acquainted with a total order without the temporal sequence of past, present and future. For Avicenna, as for the Stoics, such a kind of knowledge has certainty (yaqīnī, cf. the Stoic doctrine that πίστις belongs to the Sage only [*Stoic. Vet. Frag.* III, 147, 18 etc.]) because, thanks to the unalterable chain of causes and effects, every event is fixed and necessary. Alexander of Aphrodisias, on the other hand, contends that not all events are pre-determined. But instead of rejecting fore-knowledge of such 'events', he holds that these are foreknown by God (and the prophets) as possibles only (*De Fato ap. Scripta Minora,* ed. Bruns, p. 201).

11. We see at this point the meaning of Avicenna's doctrine of confidence and certainty. An ordinary man has first to acquire a certain *habitus* or skill in a certain profession so that he becomes confident of doing original and creative thinking in that field and thereby, by the aid of the Active Intelligence, discovers new truths in that particular field. The prophet, on the other hand, already possesses a capacity which is of the order of the intellect *in habitu*. He already possesses an assurance, so that by the aid of the Active Intelligence he can create all knowledge by himself and at a stroke. Again, whereas an ordinary mind cannot know all the relations between things since its knowledge is piecemeal, the prophet has all the relations at once present in his mind. This is not merely a quantitative difference but a qualitative one. The most glaring difference will be in the sphere of law and morality, as we shall see. It is the prophet alone, who seeing the nature of the whole course of history at a glance, is able to create moral values and to embody them in legal prescriptions.

12. This despite the fact that in the Psychology of the *Shifā'* the Intellect and the Soul of the Universe are sharply distinguished: mark the shifting terminology.

13. The idea of common, self-evident notions is, of course, Stoic.

14. This is identical with the 'third faculty of the soul' mentioned at the beginning of the quotation: mark how the Active or the Angelic Intellect is described both as a 'part of the soul' and as existing in the soul not essentially but only accidentally.

15. cf. al-Fārābī, *Siyāsāt* (pp. 49, 19–50, 2): 'Then there emanates from the Active Intelligence into the passive (human) intellect a faculty (or power) by which (man, i.e. the prophet) understands the moral-legal values of things and acts and can correctly put them in the service of ultimate happiness, thanks to this emanation . . . which is Revelation.'

16. The passage is in Avicenna's *Risāla fī Ithbāt al-Nubuwwāt* (in *Tis' Rasā'il*, Cairo, 1326 A.H.), p. 121–17, p. 124, 3.

17. Aristotle himself is not very clear as to the relation between the 'intellect which makes all things' and 'the intellect which becomes all things' in his discussion of the distinction between two intellects in *De An.*, III, 5. Later, Alexander of Aphrodisias identified the Active Intellect with God, not being very faithful to the actual language of his master (e.g. 'in the soul,' 'when separated'). For the Stoics, who took popular religious notions into their philosophy, the guiding principle of

each man is his daimon. One can ask questions of it and hear answers
from it (*Epictetus*, iii, 22, 53; Plutarch, *De Gen. Socr.*, 20). For Plutarch,
the real man is outside the empirical man, transcending his rational soul
and is to be called Daimon and not NOUS, for what exists in the rational
soul is not knowledge but only reflections in a mirror. (See the quotation
from *De Gen. Socr.* in Chap. I.). Here we see clearly that the Daimon is
distinguished from the empirical man but identified with the ideal man:
that which directs and guides the former *is* the latter.

For Plotinus the daimon is always the relatively superior principle for
what is under its guidance and direction (*Enn.* III, 4); for the sage, who
represents the pinnacle of humanity, the daimon is therefore none other
than the intelligible God (*Enn.* III, 4, 6), or the NOUS itself. This NOUS
possesses the real intelligibles; the soul possesses only the traces of these
intelligibles and in contemplation must, therefore, have recourse to these
real ones. The stages by which this is reached are (1) the purification,
(2) the 'return' or conversion towards the NOUS, (3) contemplation;
(*Enn.* I, ii, 4): εἶχε δὲ (ἡ ψυχή) οὐκ αὐτά, ἀλλὰ τύπους· δεῖ οὖν τὸν τύπον τοῖς
ἀληθινοῦς, ὧν καὶ οἱ τύποι, ἐφαρμόσαι. Τάχα δὲ καὶ οὕτω λέγεται ἔχειν,
ὅτι ὁ νοῦς ἀλλότριος καὶ μάλιστα δὲ οὐκ ἀλλότριος, ὅταν πρὸς αὐτὸν βλέπῃ.
The NOUS therefore becomes 'ours' in contemplation, even though it
is not so when we do not contemplate it. It is in this latter sense that
Plotinus denies (*Enn.* V, iii, 3) that the NOUS is a part of the soul.
Indeed, according to Plotinus what we 'are' or our self changes at different
levels depending on what our guiding principle is.

In any case, the Muslim philosophical tradition of revelation does not
envisage that total 'otherness' of the giver of revelation which is characteristic of the Semitic tradition. This total 'otherness' was safeguarded by
Philo who regarded revelation as a suspension or suppression of the
prophet's self by God or by a divine agent (see his *Quis rer.* 249 sq.);
and he seems to have safeguarded it in order to establish the purity of
verbal revelation. The Muslim philosophers regard revelation not as a
suppression of the prophet's personality but as its enlargement, an
enlargement which already lies potentially in the prophet and which,
when actualized, makes him a member of the ideal world. Therefore,
they had to seek other philosophical methods in order to make possible
verbal revelation and the appearance of the angel, as we shall see in
the next section.

18. Plato, *Phd.* 80 a; (the soul) resembles God (at its highest stage);
it is θεοειδέσ τι (ibid. 95 c); in *Rep.* 500 d, the true philosopher is θεῖος;
'according to me, man is never God (θεός) but Divine (θεῖος) and I give
this name to all (true) philosophers' (*Soph.* 216 b). The Hermetist
describes such a man as ὁ τοῦ θεοῦ δεκτικὸς καὶ τῷ θεῷ συνουσιαστικός

(i.e. an associate of God = Walīy Allāh), lib. XII, 19. This is very common in later neo-Platonic circles. The Stoics also believed that the μαντική brings mortals near to the divine powers, Cicero, op. cit. I, 1: magnifica quidem res et salutaris . . . quaque proxime ad deorum vim natura mortalis possit accedere; so Synesius, de Insomniis 1: τῷ μὲν γὰρ εἰδέναι, καὶ ὅλως τῷ γνωστικῷ τῆς δυνάμενως, θεός τε ἀνθρώπου καὶ ἄνθρωπος διαφέρει θηρίου. ἀλλὰ θεῷ μὲν εἰς τὸ γινώσκειν ἡ φύσις ἀρκεῖ· ἀπὸ δὲ μαντείας ἀνθρώπῳ πολλαπλάσιον παραγίνεται τοῦ τῇ κοινῇ φύσει προσήκοντος; also Iamblichus, de Myst., II, xi.

The term 'Divine Pneuma (rūḥ al-Qudus) is immediately Christian; but the idea that 'enthusiasm' occurred by 'inspiration' i.e. the influx of the divine pneuma or breath is old, cf. Democritus, Fragment 18, Diels; Ps.–Plato, Axiochus 370 c: εἰ μή τι θεῖον ὄντως ἐνῆν πνεῦμα τῇ ψυχῇ δι' οὗ τὴν τῶν τηλικῶνδε περίνοιαν καὶ γνῶσιν ἔσχεν; Plutarch, De Exil., XIII: τὸ ἱερὸν καὶ δαιμόνιονὲν Μούσαις πνεῦμα.

19. The Stoics themselves rejected the idea of a direct Divine Finger in the production of prophecy (Cic. De. Div. I, 118): non placet Stoicis singulis jecorum fissis aut avium cantibus interesse deum. On the other hand, they did not, as has been said, allow a universal, total knowledge of causal chain to any man, hence they stuck to the Greek conception of the 'seer' who, by a rational interpretation of signs could have a foreknowledge of events.

20. Pythagoras, Plato, Aristotle etc., were accepted as prophets by al-Fārābī and Avicenna (For al-Fārābī see Taḥṣil al-Saʿāda, last paragraph; for Avicenna see e.g. Tisʿ Ras. pp. 124, 17–25, 1.

21. See Van den Bergh, Averroes' Tahāfut al-Tahāfut (London, 1954), Vol. II, last note. The Stoics gave as examples of their Divines (θεῖοι), Socrates, Diogenes, Antisthenes; see Diog. L., VII, 91. The tendency to look upon the great personages of the past as great philosophers is already in Plato. The Stoics looked upon their heroes as embodiments of all possible virtue and greatness, see e.g. Cicero De Off., iii, 4, 16. The Stoics were especially pressed to give examples because of their absolutely idealistic conception of the Sage.

As regards the different capacities of souls, it is illuminating to compare this doctrine with that of Plotinus who explains the differences in the 'ruling' or 'commanding' capacities of souls in the following manner (Enn. IV, iii, 6): ἢ θαυμαστὸν οὐδὲν τοὺς τὴν αὐτὴν ἐπιστήμην ἔχοντας τοὺς μὲν πλειόνων, τοὺς δὲ ἐλαττόνων ἄρχειν. ἀλλὰ διὰ τί εἰπεῖν ἄν ἔχοι τις. ἀλλ' ἔστιν, εἴποι τις ἄν, καὶ ψυχῶν διαφορὰ ᾗ μᾶλλον, καθὸ ἡ μὲν οὐκ ἀπέστη τῆς ὅλης, ἀλλ' ἔσχεν ἐκεῖ οὖσα περὶ αὐτὴν τὸ σῶμα, αἱ δὲ ἤδη ὄντος, οἷον ἀδελφῆς ψυχῆς ἀρχούσης μοίρας διέλαχον . . . ἔστι δὲ καὶ τὴν μὲν πρὸς τὸν ὅλον νοῦν ἰδεῖν, τὰς δὲ μᾶλλον πρὸς τοὺς αὐτῶν τοὺς ἐν μέρει. The difference is that the one has not abandoned the Universal Soul, the others have; the one contemplates the entire Intelligence, the others only partial ones.

22. Iamblichus (Stobaeus 1, 363, 6) distinguishes between 'morphotic' and 'amorphotic' kinds of knowledge. Proclus says that the faculty of imagination transforms into symbols and images the pure intellectual truth: ἑνὸς γὰρ ὄντος τοῦ μετεχομένου θεοῦ νοῦς μὲν ἄλλως μεταλαμβάνει, ψυχὴ δὲ ἄλλως νοερά, φαντασία δὲ ἄλλως, αἴσθησις δὲ ἄλλως. ὁ μὲν ἀμερίστως, ἡ δὲ ἀνειλιγμένως, ἡ δὲ μορφωτικῶς, ἡ δὲ παθητικῶς (in Remp. I, III, 19 sq.), cf. the anonymous περὶ ἀπίστων (in Mythographi Graeci iii, Leipzig, 1902, ed. N. Festa): ἡ φαντασία . . . μορφωτικῶς (θεοῦ) μετέχει. Again, Proclus, ibid, 235, 18: καὶ ἡ μὲν φαντασία νόησις οὖσα μορφωτικὴ νοητῶν ἐθέλει γνῶσις εἶναι τινων. Proclus complains (ibid, 74, 26) that the Christian critics of the pagan religion follow only its morphotic symbols instead of its pure intellectual meaning. The doctrine that the Greek religious myths represented in symbolic form the higher philosophical religious truth for the masses was already defended by the Stoics as we shall see later (see also S. Van den Bergh, op. cit. II, p. 98). But the inner psychological explanation of this symbolizing process was, it seems, achieved only in neo-Platonism and, most probably, by Iamblichus. For Proclus, the idea that imagination expresses morphotically the higher spiritual truth is only one aspect of, or rather, a corollary of his general principle that 'all things are in all things but in each according to its own nature' (see his *Elements of Theology*, ed. E. R. Dodds, Oxford, 1933, proposition 193 etc.), a principle which may well have ultimately come from the Stoic doctrine of 'Sympatheia'.

23. Al-Fārābī, *Madina*, pp. 49–50; Avicenna, *Shifā*, Psychology, IV, 2. For a fuller account of this function of suggestion see below, section 3.

24. Al-Fārābī, *Madina*, p. 49.

25. Al-Fārābī, op cit., Avicenna, op cit.

26. Greek philosophers had insistently held that prophecy occurred in dreams because of the withdrawal of the soul from the world of sense, see e.g. Cicero, *De Div.* I, 49; I, 57 etc.; Plutarch, *Def. Orac.*, 48; *De Pyth Orac.*, 21–23; already Plutarch emphasizes in this last book that the Revelation is a product of the interaction of two factors, the divine and the human, and represents the human soul as a limiting factor: the soul,

he says, is the organ and medium of divine Revelation and as such cannot fail to colour it; more fully, see below, the question of verbal Revelation.

27. cf. Plutarch, *de Gen. Socr.*, XX, where we are told that the Daimon speaks in us all the time but we do not hear it because we are engrossed in the tumult of the external world. Plutarch says that many people believe that the Daimon can come to us in dreams but they regard it impossible that this could occur in waking life. He contends that if our souls are sufficiently pure and quiet so that conditions of withdrawal obtain, Revelation could come to them equally when they are awake: οὗτως οἱ τῶν δαιμόνων λόγοι διὰ πάντων φερόμενοι, μόνοις ἐνηχοῦσι τοῖς ἀθόρυβον ἦθος καὶ νήνεμον ἔχουσι τὴν ψυχήν· οὓς δὴ καὶ ἱεροὺς καὶ δαιμονίους ἀνθρώπους καλοῦμεν. οἱ δὲ πολλοὶ καταδαρθοῦσιν οἴονται τὸ δαιμόνιον ἀνθρώποις ἐπιθειάζειν. εἰ δ' ἐγρηγορότας καὶ καθεστῶτας ἐν τῷ φρονεῖν ὁμοίως κινοῦσι, θαυμαστὸν ἡγοῦνται καὶ ἄπιστον . . . τὸ γὰρ αἴτιον οὐ συνορῶσι, τὴν ἐν αὐτοῖς ἀναρμοστίαν καὶ ταραχήν, ἧς ἀπήλλακται Σωκράτης, ὁ ἑταῖρος ἡμῶν. See also Cic., op. cit., I, 51.

28. This account of this peculiar case of vision in its formal characteristics rests on the Platonic type of the theory of vision as developed by Posei-donius on the basis of the relation of sympathy that holds between the mind and the outside world in all perceptual experience. According to this theory, what we perceive we already possess in ourselves also and perception takes place on the basis of this con-naturalness (συμφυία) of the inner and the outer worlds. For Poseidonius' theory see, e.g. *Sextus Empiricus, Adversus Math.*, VII, 92–109, 116–119 and 128–33. For the substance of the theory see below Plutarch's account in n. 31.

29. Al-Fārābī, *Madīna*, pp. 51, 14–52, 12.

30. Avicenna, *Shifā', Psychology*, V, 6 (and the corresponding text of the *Najāt*): 'It is not improbable that some of these actions attributed to the Holy Spirit overflow, because of their exalted and overwhelming force, to the imaginative faculty which then figurizes them into visual and acoustic symbols in the manner indicated above.' The passage to which this quotation refers is *Shifā', Psychology*, IV, 2: 'Often an apparition presents itself to them and they imagine that what they are (inwardly, mentally) perceiving is an actual address from that apparition in verbal forms actually heard, preserved and recited. This is the prophecy peculiar to the imaginative faculty.' (It should be incidentally noted that the words 'in the manner indicated above' also occur in the corresponding passage of the *Najāt* even though the passage to which they refer is not to be found in that work. This fact is some comment on the manner of the composition of the *Najāt*).

31. cf. the last of the two quotations in the preceding note. More fully, ibid: 'When it happens through some cause or other—either through the activity of the imagination or the intellect (fikr) or the configurations (tashakkulāt) of the heavenly bodies—that a form impresses itself on the faculty of representation (muṣawwira), while the mind is not taking notice of it, it can impress itself (directly) in the *sensus communis* itself. Then the subject hears voices and sees colours (i.e. objects) which have no existence in the external world nor are their causes from the outside.'

32. The phenomena of apparitions and voices were common part of prophecy in Greco-Roman philosophy. See e.g. Cic. op cit., I, XLV; also Plutarch, *de Def. Orac.*, 17, where it is related how the divine voice addressed to an Egyptian pilot was heard by all on the boat, 'Pan the Great is dead.' Plutarch, however, holds that normally verbal revelation as such does not occur: that the words are not the production of direct divine agency which only supplies the inspiration which then the prophet himself translates into verbal form: 'Let us not believe that the God has composed these (prophetic utterances): he only provides the origin of enthusiasm and then the prophetic priestesses are moved each in accordance with her natural faculties. Certainly, if it were necessary to write the oracles, instead of delivering them orally, I do not think that we should believe the handwriting to be the God's. . . . As a matter of fact, the voice is not that of a god, nor the utterance of it, nor the diction, nor the metre, but all these are the woman's; he puts into her mind only the images (φαντασίας) and creates a light in her soul. . . .' (*de. Pyth. Orac.*, 7). Plutarch returns to this theme again and again, cf. ibid. 20; *de. Def. Orac.*, 9: 'Certainly, it would be foolish and childish in the extreme to imagine that the God himself, after the manner of ventriloquists . . . enters into the bodies of his prophets and prompts their utterances, employing their mouths and voices as instruments.' The verbal revelation, then, is a sort of collaboration between the divine and the human agencies. This position with regard to the verbal revelation stands in direct opposition to that of Philo (see above n. 17). The Muslim philosophers' doctrine about the verbal revelation seems to be midway between these two views.

In his *de Gen. Socr.*, XX, again, Plutarch, after stating that the inspiration given to Socrates by his demon was not something visual but audible, says: ὥσπερ καὶ καθ' ὕπνον οὐκ ἔστι φωνή, λόγων δέ τινων δόξας καὶ νοήσεις λαμβάνοντες, οἴονται φθεγγομένων ἀκούειν. Thus, just as in dreams one does not really hear voices but thinks that one does, so in waking revelation. The demon does not actually speak to the prophet but without sound touches his intellect and deposits the 'meaning' (τὸ δηλούμενον) therein. This is based on the sympathy among the pure souls. Even in ordinary human communication, Plutarch goes on, the words really only

C*

serve as a blow to make the mind attentive ($\pi\lambda\eta\gamma\grave{\eta}$ $\tau\hat{\eta}s$ $\psi\upsilon\chi\hat{\eta}s$) or as a token, the real intercourse existing only between souls, thanks to the sympathy existing between them. Now, the pure souls which are not drowned in the bodily tumult do not need this blow.

Nevertheless, Plutarch admits the possibility of verbal revelation 'in order to convince those who lack faith.' His conception of this process, although not quite identical with that of al-Fārābī's, is strikingly similar: 'The air, when "informed" by clear and articulate sounds (by sympathy-these words also occur in Philo, *Decal*, 9, 33), and changed entirely into voice, communicates the thoughts to the mind of the hearer. It is therefore not to be wondered at if, for this reason, the air becomes easily impressionable to the thoughts of a pure (demonic) mind, and (having been "informed" by them) reports them to the divine and extraordinary individuals.' In this case the verbal symbols will b: as much a direct product of the divine agency as the spiritual inspiration itself.

Compare with this double-aspect (spiritual and perceptual) account of revelation what Avicenna says (*Tis' Rasā'il*, p. 66,12–67, 10), 'Angels have real and absolute being but also a being relative to human beings. Their real being is in the transcendental realm and is contacted only by the holy human spirits. When the two meet, the human being's both senses—internal and external—are attracted upwards and the angel is presented to them in accordance with the power of the man who sees the angel not in the absolute but the relative form. He hears the latter's speech ($=\lambda\acute{o}\gamma os$) *as* a voice even though it is intrinsically a spiritual communication (waḥy). Spiritual communication is the indication of the mind of the angel to the human spirit in a direct manner—and this is the real 'speech'. For speech is only that which brings home the meaning of the addressor's mind (to the addressee's mind) so that the latter becomes like the former.

'Where the addressor cannot touch the mind of the addressee directly in the manner in which a seal touches a piece of wax and cannot render it like itself (as in the case of ordinary human communication), it takes an exterior ambassador—like voice, writing or gesticulation.

'But where the addressee is a (pure) mind so that there is no veil between it and the addressor's mind, the latter shines upon the former as the sun shines upon clear water and his mind is impressed by an impression which then overflows also in the internal sense (i.e. imagination) and when it is very strong, it impresses itself on it so that it is perceived (visibly and audibly). Thus the recipient of revelation contacts the angel by his interior (mind) and receives revelation internally, but the angel also appears to him in a visual form and his speech takes on an audible form. In this way, the angel and the revelation come to his cognitive faculties in both ways (i.e. spiritual and imaginative–perceptual).'— the treatise of Avicenna from which this quotation is taken forms part of the treatise *Fuṣūṣ al-Ḥikam* attributed to al-Fārābī (*Dieterici*, pp. 72, 13–79, 11); see chap. I, n. 2, also p. 85, 10.

33. *Najāt*, p. 302, sq.: There are three ways in which the heavenly bodies influence earthly events; one of these is through the images in their souls; line 6, 'It has become clear to you that the souls of these heavenly bodies have a certain manipulation in particular images in that they possess a knowledge not purely rational, whereby they attain to a knowledge of particular events. This is rendered possible for them by knowing the interactions of the active and the passive causes of these events and what is to emerge from these causes. . . . (line 17) Now, the conglomeration and interaction of all these processing causes constitute a system under the sway of the movement of the Spheres. Since the Primary Substances (i.e. Pure Intelligences) know these events and since these Substances necessarily produce the Secondary Substances (i.e. the heavenly bodies), it follows that these latter come to know these events as well. That is how we know that the souls of the heavenly bodies and the higher Substances know the particulars. As for the higher Substances, they know these in a universal manner, but the heavenly bodies know them as particulars and as (perceptually) experienced or quasi (perceptually) experienced. The heavenly bodies, then, necessarily know what is to happen'. Avicenna then affirms on the following page (line 15 sq.) that the souls of the heavenly bodies transmit this knowledge of particular future events to the saints or mystics by *ilhām*, i.e. by an inspiration of the particular.

It seems to me clear from this account that Avicenna is not speaking here of prophecy proper but only of the visions of the mystics. Al-Ghazālī, however, in his *Tahāfut*, represents this mode of fore-knowledge as covering both *Waḥy* and *ilhām*, for which I find no support in Avicenna (see n. 34).

Sometimes, as in *Shifāʾ*, *Psychology*, IV, 2, this influence is attributed to 'heavenly configuration.' For this purely imaginative prophecy see Plutarch, *de Def. Orac.*, 40: 'But that which foretells the future, like an unwritten tablet, being irrational and indeterminate in itself, but receptive of images and presentiments, unreasoningly grasps the future. . . .'; see Van den Bergh, op. cit., II, pp. 165–6; cf. also Porphyry (ap. *Eusebius Praep. Evang.*, VI, 5). The doctrine of the influence of the heavenly bodies and events on sublunary things is very common especially in later Hellenism and in fact the doctrine that heavenly events indicate earthly course of events is only a special case of this doctrine; see especially Iamblichus' *Life of Pythagoras*, 218, where the dependence of earthly events on heavenly events is discussed.

34. This is the theory which al-Ghazālī attacks in the 16th discussion of

his *Refutation of Philosophy* to which Averroes replied by saying that this theory of prophecy is peculiarly Avicennian.

35. There seems to run through all the account of imaginative prophecy a contradiction, viz. that on the one hand, the prophet is required to have such a strong imagination that the intellect is unable to control it, and on the other, that imagination should be at rest or controlled by reason in order to record—as faithfully as it can—the higher truth. This contradiction is already in Plutarch, if one compares his two accounts given above in notes 32 and 33 respectively, for in the one case the account points to a rational prophecy, in the other to a professedly irrational one. This contradiction appears more glaring in Avicenna because his account is more detailed but would be equally applicable to al-Fārābī. Avicenna tries to come to terms with this a little later in the same chapter when he says, 'Among those who see these things in waking life, some do so because of the exaltedness of their souls and their strong imaginative and memorative powers . . . while others do so because of their lack of *rational discernment* so that their imagination is very strong and they can receive the Unseen in waking life.' But further on in the same passage he reverts to his contention that a cessation both of perceptual and intellectual activity is necessary in order to receive imaginative revelation. It is quite clear that these men actually have concrete cases of both types in mind, only they are unable to devise a theory which would do justice to their facts.

36. Avicenna, *Shifāʾ*, *Psychology*, IV, 2; cf. also al-Fārābī, *Madīna*, p. 48, 20sq.

37. If this line of thought is pursued alone—as is often done by all the three great philosophers of Islam—the doctrine certainly rests on the assumption (not, however, conscious, and certainly not admitted expressly) of a pious fraud, i.e. a political manoeuvre of mankind for a good end by a shrewd and good man through deliberate pious lies. When, however, this approach is combined with the compulsory Law of Symbolization, described before, the picture is considerably modified. Indeed, it disappears if the compulsory Law of Symbolization is seriously taken, for it would then mean that the prophet himself believes in the *truth* of symbols just as much as he believes in the truth of the spiritual inspiration. Actually, however, these philosophers do not often do so: 'When these contemplative and practical virtues come to exist by themselves (i.e. not figuratively) in the mind of the Lawgiver, they constitute philosophy, while in the minds of the masses they are religion (milla should be read throughout for malaka; cf. below n. 93). . . . In the mind of the Lawgiver himself too, these figurizations exist, but not as images and persuasions. . . . It is, indeed, he who has *invented* these images and persuasive symbols *not in order to understand himself the higher realities as a religion but as symbols and*

images for others' (al-Fārābī, *Taḥṣil-al-Saʿāda*, p. 44). *Religion*, then, exists only for the masses, for the prophet himself only the highest prize of philosophy. See also Avicenna, *Tisʿ Rasāʾil*, p. 124 sq.

38. Al-Fārābī, *Siyāsāt*, pp. 55–56.

39. See e.g. *Najāt*, p. 305, 21 sq. 'The prophet's message may, indeed, contain allusions and hints to invite those capable by nature to delve into deeper wisdom concerning the ways of worship and their benefits for this life and the hereafter.' See also Averroes *Tahāfut al-Tahāfut*, p. 582, 11 sq. The doctrine of the Muslim philosophers that a part of the Holy Book should be allegorically interpreted because it contains certain clear suggestions of the spiritual truth, rests immediately on the *Koran*, III, 6: 'It is He who has sent down the Book to thee containing verses which are firm and are the Mother of the Book, and others which are ambiguous. Those in whose hearts there is perversity follow the ambiguous part seeking (to sow) sedition and to misinterpret; but its interpretation no one knows except Allah and those firm in knowledge.' There is a controversy in Islam, however, whether the latter kind of verses are to be interpreted or not: the extreme orthodox wing of Islam disallows delving into the interpretation of these 'ambiguous' verses and they put a full stop after the word 'Allah' in the above quotation so as to exclude 'those firm in knowledge' from understanding them. The more liberal, however, including many moderate orthodox ulema, allow interpretation and do not stop at the word 'Allah' so as to include 'those firm in knowledge' among the category of those who can understand. The doctrine must have arisen out of an attempt to justify so many arbitrary allegorical interpretations—the Shi'ite, the mystical and the philosophical. The practice of allegorization on this kind of basis is, of course, very old. The Greeks when thus interpreting Homer, saw in his poetry a part which told the pure truth while the other part concealed this truth under the guise of popular imagery (*Stoic Vet. Frag.* I, 63, 9 sq.): ὁ δὲ Ζήνων οὐδὲν τῶν τοῦ Ὁμήρου ψέγει, ἅμα διηγούμενος καὶ διδάσκων ὅτι τὰ μὲν κατὰ δόξαν, τὰ δὲ κατὰ ἀλήθειαν γέγραφεν, ὅπως μὴ φαίνεται αὐτὸς αὑτῷ μαχόμενος. . . . ὁ δὲ λόγος οὗτος ᾿Αντισθένους ἐστι πρότερον, ὅτι τὰ μὲν δόξῃ, τὰ δὲ ἀληθείᾳ. . . . Right in the wake of this procedure, then, followed the Jewish (see *Philo, Immut II, Somn*, 1, 40), the Christian and the Muslim allegorists.

40. This universalism with regard to the spirit of religions is Stoic; the Stoics deduced the idea of cosmopolitanism directly from their doctrine of 'Common Notions'. See e.g. *Marcus Aurelius* IV, 4: εἰ τὸ νοερὸν ἡμῖν κοινόν, καὶ ὁ λόγος, καθ᾽ ὃν λογικοί ἐσμεν, κοινός. εἰ τοῦτο, καὶ ὁ προστακτικὸς

τῶν ποιητέων ἢ μὴ λόγος κοινός. cf. also al-Fārābī, *Siyāsāt*, p. 50, last paragraph.

41. See also Averroes, op. cit., p. 583 where he enjoins that one must follow the best religion of his times and says that this is why the teachers of philosophy at Alexandria became Muslims, just as in other places they had become Christians. Al-Fārābī and Averroes, while maintaining the superiority of Islam in religious symbolism, do not, to my knowledge, derogate any other religion by name. Avicenna, however, has attacked Magianism and Manicheaism (*R. Aḍḥawiya*, p. 54) and Christianity (ibid, p. 61): The former are accused of producing an unintelligible symbolism (light and darkness). Against Christianity it is urged that its symbolism is ineffective. The question concerns the resurrection of the body. If, Avicenna says, you regard the body as man or as part of man, then, of course, you must believe in the resurrection of the body; but then why not speak of bodily happiness and unhappiness? If, on the other hand, happiness and unhappiness are purely spiritual, what is the sense in affirming bodily resurrection?

42. The procedure of the allegorical interpretation of the materialistic symbols of popular belief goes far back into Hellenism but its wholesale application was made in the Stoic School. The Stoic philosophy undertook the task of interpretation and protection of the popular religion based on Homer and Hesiod. These poets, in the course of time, had come to be looked upon as depositories of the religious truth and were venerated. See above n. 39 about Zeno's estimate of Homer. Indeed, Homer was venerated as an immortal god (see Eusebius, *Praep. Evang.*, V. 33). Even poetry in general came to be regarded by the Stoics as an attribute of the Sage. H. A. Wolfson's attempt (see his *Philo*, Vol. I, p. 138–9) to differentiate radically between the Greeks' approach to the popular religion and that of Philo to the Jewish Scriptures does not seem to me justified as it stands. Of course, as we have said already, Philo looks upon Scriptures as the literal Word of God (and this characteristic extends, according to him, even to their Greek version), but as mentioned before, this does not prevent him from saying that God's word uses anthropomorphic symbols for the sake of the masses and conceals the higher truth. So did the Greeks with Homer and Hesiod (see n. 39). Again, Wolfson says (op. cit., II, 128), 'Then, again, in Greek religion, the objections to anthropomorphisms on philosophic grounds led either to a rejection of the popular deities altogether, or to a transformation, by the allegorical method, of the popular deities, into philosophic entities or concepts.' This obviously did not happen with Judaism for the objections to anthropomorphisms 'merely led to the general explanation that anthropomorphic

expressions are not to be taken literally and that they are used in Scripture only as a practical, pedagogical device. . . .' On the contrary, the Stoics sought to keep the popular religion at the popular level: witness, e.g. Epictetus, *Diss*, II, 20, 32, sq., where he accuses those who challenge or cast doubt on popular deities, of robbing the common man of the only force which keeps him from evil. Wolfson's approach throughout the book seems to me imbued with a nationalistic sentiment which, if not duly kept in check, is liable to sway the intellectual honesty and sense of proportion. Indeed, in the opening lines of his book Wolfson declares that 'with a single exception, none of the peoples who after the conquests of Alexander began to participate in Greek philosophy contributed anything radically new to it' including the founder of the Stoic school. Wolfson maintains (op. cit., I, 143 sq.) that the subjugation of philosophy to theology was a uniquely original stroke of Philo—and he ignores the entire religious trend of Stoic and post-Stoic philosophy.

43. See the reference to Epictetus in the last note. So Philo, *de Abr.*, 29, 36, 41, etc. Esotericism became very prominent in neo-Platonism and Gnosticism.

44. See, however, n. 39 above.

45. Avicenna is referring here to such verses as 'Nothing is like Him' (*Kor.* 42, 11) on which the Muslim rationalists and philosophers base their allegorizations, and on the Old Testament equivalents of which Philo had based his (*Num.* 23).

46. e.g. the resurrection of the bodies.

47. *Kor.* 2, 210.

48. Ibid, 6, 159.

49. Iḍmār is a figure in Arabic rhetoric meaning the suppression of a word or a phrase (so that the speaker keeps it in his heart) on the assumption that it will be understood by the addressee.

50. *Kor.* 48, 10.

51. Ibid, 39, 56.

52. *Ishārāt*, III, p. 252, 12.

80 PROPHECY IN ISLAM

53. Sextus Empiricus, *Adv. Math*, IX, 79.

54. Above pp. 35, 67.

55. See e.g. *Marcus Aurelius*, VI, 38, where the words φιλία, σύμπνοια and τονικὴ κίνησις are used to describe the mutual relationship of things.

56. See above p. 73, 35, quotation from Plutarch; *Cicero, De Div.*, II, 14, 34, etc., Zeller's statement (*Phil. d. Griechen*, III, 1, 5th edition, p. 172, note 2), that the Stoic conception of Sympathy did not really go beyond a natural, physical connection would not seem quite correct.

57. See the reference to Sext. Emp. in note 53 above; also Epictetus, *Diss.*, I, 14: συμπαθεῖν τὰ ἐπίγεια τοῖς οὐρανίοις οὐ δοκεῖ σοι;.Λοκεῖ ἔφη.

58, *Enn.*, IV, 4, 32: συμπαθὲς δὴ πᾶν τοῦτο τὸ ἕν, καὶ ὡς ζῷον ἕν, καὶ τὸ πόρρωδὴ ἐγγύς . . . ἀλλὰ διαλείποντος τοῦ μεταξὺ καὶ παθόντος οὐδὲν, ἔπαθε τὸ οὐκ ἐγγύς. οὐ γὰρ ἐφεξῆς τῶν ὁμοίων κειμένων, διειλημμένων δὲ ἑτέροις μεταξύ, τῇ δὲ ὁμοιότητι συμπασχόντων, καὶ εἰς τὸ πόρρω ἀφικεῖσθαι ἀνάγκη τὸ παρὰ τοῦ μὴ παρακειμένου δρώμενον, ζῷον τε ὄντος καὶ εἰς ἓν τελοῦντος οὐδὲν οὕτω πόρρω τόπῳ, ὡς μὴ ἐγγὺς εἶναι τῇ τοῦ ἑνὸς ζῴου πρὸς τὸ συμπαθεῖν φύσει.

59. *Enn.*, IV, 4, 34, 43, 44.

60. ibid., IV, 4, 43: πᾶν γὰρ τὸ πρὸς ἄλλο γοητεύεται ὑπ' ἄλλου· πρὸς ὃ γάρ ἐστιν, ἐκεῖνο γοητεύει καὶ ἄγει αὐτό. . . . διὸ καὶ πᾶσα πρᾶξις γεγοήτευται καὶ πᾶς ὁ τοῦ πρακτικοῦ βίος. . . . .

61. ibid., IV, 4, 41.

62. When Plotinus speaks of prayer in *Enn.*, IV, 4, 26 sq., he is thinking of external ritualistic prayers which operate through Sympathy. In V, i, 6, however, he distinguishes between an external prayer 'of words' and an inner, spiritual prayer of Ecstasis: ὧδε οὖν λεγέσθω θεὸν αὐτὸν ἐπικαλεσαμένοις οὐ λογῷ γεγωνῷ ἀλλὰ τῇ ψυχῇ ἐκτείνασιν ἑαυτοὺς εἰς εὐχὴν πρὸς ἐκεῖνον, εὔχεσθαι τὸν τρόπον τοῦτον δυναμένους μόνους πρὸς μόνον.

63. According to Porphyry, ritualistic prayers and theurgic processes are of no intellectual and spiritual benefit, although they bring the irrational and physical impulses in contact with demons and angels: Augustine, *De Civitate Dei*, X, 9: nam et Porphyrius quandam quasi purgationem animae per theurgiam, cunctanter tamen et pudibunda

quodammodo disputatione promittit; reversionem vero ad Deum hanc artem praestare cuiquam negat . . . nunc autem velut ejus laudatoribus cedens, utilem dicit esse mundandae parti animae, non quidem intellect-uali, qua rerum intelligibilium percipitur veritas nullas habentium similitudines corporum; sed spiritali, qua corporalium rerum capiuntur imagines etc.

64. This line of thought, if pursued vigorously, might conceivably have led Avicenna to make this earthly body worthy of an after-life, at least for a certain class of people, viz. those whose bodily passions had come to conform with spiritual demands and he might not have given a violent affront to orthodox Islam. But his Greek legacy of a radical metaphysical and moral antithesis between the body and the soul, according to which matter is inherently not-being and evil, prevented him from doing so. The nearest of the philosophical opinions to the orthodox view concerning the physical tortures and pleasures of after-life, is the one described by Avicenna towards the end of *R. Aḍḥawīa* (pp. 124–25). Undeveloped souls, he states there as being the opinion of some philosophers, without himself confirming or denying it, survive with their irrational physical impulses and imagination and so may, after death, experience the pleasures and pains which they would experience if the body had actually survived: 'Some scholars say that when the soul leaves the body and carries the imaginative faculty along with it . . . it is impossible for it to be absolutely free from the body. . . . It then imagines that it is experiencing pains by way of usual physical chastisements, and, all that it used to believe during its earthly life, would happen to it after death. . . . These scholars say that it is not impossible that the soul should (also) imagine an agreeable state of affairs and that it should experience, in after-life, all that is mentioned in the prophets' Revelations—Gardens and houries, etc.' (wa-aʻtaqid-uhū, in the last but one line of this passage should be read as waʻtaqadahū, since Avicenna is only reporting somebody else's opinion). The idea, however, that at least in the cases of undeveloped souls, the irrational part survives and pain and pleasure (or only pain?) follow as chas-tisements (and rewards?), is affirmed by Plotinus; see *Enn.* I, 10, 6; IV, 7, 14 (where it is said that only in the case of unpurified souls the irrational impulses survive). The doctrine is also in Porphyry according to whom the soul leaves the physical body in a pneumatic encasement which it slowly discards during ascent—an idea which Avicenna, who attributes it to Thābit ibn Qurra, rejects in the last sentence of this work.

65. *Ishārāt*, III, p. 250, 10–251, 5: 'People of certain natural dispositions seek the aid of certain actions (in the production of prophetic knowledge) through which their perceptual faculty is struck with a sense of wonder

(ḥaira) and their imagination with astonishment, so that their faculty of receiving the Unseen becomes ready to receive it well (i.e. because of the withdrawal of the soul from the external world). . . . For example, it is related about a Turcoman tribe that when they go to consult their soothsayer for some prophecy, he begins to run around very rapidly and keeps on gasping until he faints. In that state then he utters what comes into his mind; his utterances are recorded by his hearers in their memory and they erect their future plans according to them. Again, some people from whom prophecies are sought gaze constantly at something bright and quivering, so that their eyes are overpowered both by rapid quivering and by exceeding brightness. . . . This is an artificial compulsion (of the senses to 'withdraw') in order to get a brief opportunity to contact the Unseen. People especially amenable to this inducement are those who are by nature suggestible to a state of awe and astonishment and who can easily accept unintelligible statements, like stupid people and children.' Thus, such contrivances do not influence the Divine Realm, but the human soul itself by inducing a kind of hypnotic state.

66. This idea would be in perfect harmony with the teachings of Plotinus, but it is not found in Plotinus who is not interested in miracles. In later neo-Platonism, however, the status of the human soul as such declined considerably and, in proportion to this, the importance of theurgic practices grew; cf. n. 71 below.

67. This account of the genesis of emotions like joy, anger, etc. grounds them ultimately in cognition and is Stoic. The Stoics define anger, e.g. as a desire to avenge oneself upon someone whom one believes to have committed an outrage against one. This is the usual line followed by Avicenna although he notes, Shifā', Psychology, III, 4, that sometimes painful bodily states, when one tries to remove their cause, generate cognitive processes. Plotinus also, Enn. IV, 4, 28, treats of anger from these two sides. It is because of the first line of thought that Avicenna regards all emotions as purely spiritual states.

68. It should be remembered that the influence of the emotional states on the body, even though stressed by Avicenna because they are more interesting, is not the only form of influence, cf. his citation of the example of an ill person who by sheer 'will-power' becomes well. Also, in the sphere of the soul's influence on other bodies, whereas some are emotional influences like jealousy operating in the case of the 'evil eye', others are voluntary, e.g. suggestion or hypnotism by concentration of the will (al-wahm al-ʿāmil). What is required by Avicenna for such an influence is a fixed idea or determination (hay'at al-ʿaqd) in the soul (Ishārāt, III, 252,

last line). For the Stoics too, the Sympathy was not restricted to involuntary emotional cases but also the voluntary rational cases of bodily movement or control are included; Plutarch, *De Virtute Morali*, 4:

'For, to be sure, even our breathing, our sinews and bones, and the other parts of the body, though they are irrational, yet when an impulse comes, with reason shaking the reins, as it were, they all grow taut and are drawn together in ready obedience. So, when a man purposes to run, his feet are keyed for action, if he purposes to throw or to grasp, his hands fall to their business. And most excellently does the poet (Homer) portray the *Sympathy* and conformity of the irrational with reason. . . .

'An evident proof of this is also the shrinking and withdrawal of the private parts, which hold their peace and remain quiet in the presence of such beautiful maidens and youths as neither reason nor law allows us to touch. . . .'

69. See Plutarch, *De Libit. et Aegr.* 6, the reference to Poseidonius' doctrine of the influence of the soul on the body. Aristotle, *De An.* I, discusses the correspondence of the mental and the physical, especially in emotional phenomena, but does not speak of the influence of the mind on the body. For him, such phenomena show that mind and body are not two substances but only one and, according to him, the physical counter-part must be included in the definition of each emotion.

70. See Plutarch, *Quaest. Conviv.* V, 7, 3 (quoted by Van den Bergh, op. cit. II, p. 174) where the influence of imagination on the excitation of sexual organs is mentioned, cf. also n. 68 above for the opposite influence of reason.

71. cf. Proclus in *Tim. Comm.* (ed. Diehl) I, p. 395, 13 (the passage has been suggested to me by R. Walzer's article 'Al-Fārābī's Theory of Prophecy and Divination' in *Hellenic Studies* 1957), where he wants to show the rational possibility of the creative activity of the Demiurge, which is timeless and needs no instruments: καὶ γὰρ οἱ τεχνῖται δέονται πρὸς τὴν ἐνέργειαν ὀργάνων διὰ τὸ μὴ πάσης κρατεῖν τῆς ὕλης, δηλοῦσι δὲ καὶ αὐτοῖς τοῖς ὀργάνοις χρώμενοι πρὸς τὸ εὐεργὸν ποιῆσαι τὴν ὕλην . . . αὐτὸς δὲ ὁ λόγος ἀχρόνως ἀπὸ τῆς Τέχνης παραγίνεται τῷ ὑποκειμένῳ, πάντων ἐξαιρεθέντων τῶν ἐμποδών. καὶ εἰ μηδὲν ἦν καὶ τούτοις ἐμπόδιον, τό τε εἶδος ἀθρόως ἂν τῇ ὕλῃ προσῆγον καὶ ὀργάνων οὐδὲν ἂν ὅλως ἐδεήθησαν. Proclus goes on to say that in the case of emotions like shame and fear imagination influences the body without any physical manipulation: καὶ μὴν καὶ ἡ φαντασία πολλὰ περὶ τὸ σῶμα παθήματα ἀπεργάζεται παρ' αὐτὴν μόνην τὴν ἑαυτῆς ἐνέργειαν . . . καὶ τὰ μὲν πάθη περὶ τὸ σῶμα, αἴτιον δὲ τούτων τὸ φάντασμα, οὐκ ὤσεσι καὶ μοχλείαις χρησάμενον, ἀλλὰ τῷ παρεῖναι

μόνον, ἐνεργῆσαν. He continues that certain super-human, demonic powers, by virtue of their powerful imagination, can work changes in nature as they like: ἔτι δὲ αὖ κατὰ τοὺς θεολόγους εἶναί τνας καὶ κρείττους ἡμῶν δυνάμεις χρωμένας δραστηρίοις φαντασίαις καὶ ἅμα τῷ γενέσθαι ποιητικαῖς, ᾧ ἂν ἐθέλωσι. . . . It is to be noted that, according to Proclus, this miracle-working efficacy belongs only to super-natural powers such as demons, the human soul can work directly only on its own body and on other bodies through its body and other instruments. According to Avicenna, on the other hand, miracle-working, even though it requires an abnormally strong soul, is nevertheless done by the soul itself, when it becomes 'a kind of world-soul.'

72. For the influence of this image on Medieval and even modern thought see S. Van den Bergh, op. cit., II, pp. 174–5.

73. This passage lays it down that, in order to be able to influence other bodies directly, a soul should not only possess a powerful constitution and will-power, but that it should be possessed of strong moral virtue. Nevertheless, as we shall see below, an evil soul can equally influence things beyond its own body, e.g. in the case of black magic and the evil eye.

74. Avicenna makes no intrinsic difference between the miracles of prophets and those of saints: the only difference is that the prophets have a natural power to perform miracles while the saints acquire this power by effort (Ishārāt, III, p. 353–4). The general tradition of Islam, however, distinguishes between the two: the miracles of the prophets are called mu'jizāt while those of the saints are called karāmāt. Even Sufis attempted a distinction. Thus al-Hujwīrī, e.g. lays down the following distinctions in his Kashf al-Mahjūb: (1) The prophet deliberately and voluntarily performs miracles as evidence of the truth of his mission, whereas the saint, since he has no socio-legal mission, does not need such evdience and therefore does not perform miracles voluntarily and purposely. (2) Hence the prophet knows that he has performed a miracle whereas the saint may not have this knowledge. Indeed, the saint sometimes does not even know whether a genuine miracle has been performed by him or whether he has been imperceptibly deceived. (3) The function of the saint's miracles is subsidiary to those of the prophet and they are only confirmatory of the latter's true mission (Nicholson's translation, pp. 218–35).

75. Ishārāt, III, p. 254. This must apparently happen when the prophet's soul, without losing individuality, becomes somehow identified with the Active Intellect—the 'Giver of Forms' to Nature as well as to the human

soul. Thus the whole created world obeys the prophet's will since the whole creation becomes his body as it were and direct Sympathy comes to exist between the two. This explains Avicenna's statement in his commentary on the pseudo-Aristotelian *Theologia* (ed. A. Badawī in his *'Aristū 'ind al-'Arab*), p. 72: 'It is not impossible that the celestial bodies should in some way be employed by souls other than their own. Especially, when a soul has perfected its power in its own body, it may, when need or expediency so demand, employ, in its place, a higher and more noble body than its own.'

It is to be noted that this explanation of miracles occurs also in Fuṣūṣ al-Ḥikam (*Haydarabād*, p. 9) attributed to al-Fārābī, who has not spoken of miracles anywhere else in his extant works: 'Peculiar to the prophet's soul is the Divine Faculty which is obeyed by the natural disposition of the created macrocosm just as your soul is obeyed by the created microcosm (i.e. your body) and so the prophet performs extraordinary miracles'.

76. *Shifā'*, *Psychology*, IV, 4.

77. According to Plotinus, the higher, contemplative mind of the sage is not vulnerable to the influence of magic but his irrational soul is, although even here magic cannot excite his amorousness, (IV, 4, 43): ὁ δὲ σπουδαῖος πῶς ὑπὸ γοητείας καὶ φαρμάκων; ἢ τῇ μὲν ψυχῇ ἀπαθὴς εἰς γοήτευσιν, καὶ οὐκ ἂν τὸ λογικὸν αὐτοῦ πάθοι, οὐδ' ἂν μεταδοξάσειε. τὸ δέ. . . . ἐν αὐτῷ ἄλογον κατὰ τοῦτο πάθοι ἄν, . . . ἀλλ' οὐκ ἔρωτας ἐκ φαρμάκων, εἴπερ τὸ ἐρᾶν ἐπινευούσης καὶ τῆς ψυχῆς τῆς ἄλλης τῷ τῆς ἄλλης παθήματι.

78. Here demons appear as departed earthly souls of men. In his *R. fī'l-ḥudūd* (in *Tis' Rasā'il*, p. 90), however, he describes a demon as 'an aery animal, possessing reason and a transparent body and capable of changing its forms', and he adds 'this is the meaning of the word, not a definition.' These last words may perhaps suggest that demons, so conceived, do not exist for Avicenna, cf. Aristotle (*Anal. Post.*) where we are told that only existing things have a definition, non-existents (e.g. centaur) cannot have an essence but in their case only the meaning of the word can be given. Al-Fārābī (R. fī Masā'il Mutafarriqa, *Haydarabad*, 1344 A.H.) defines a demon as 'an irrational, immortal animal.'

Avicenna, as usual, names no philosophers. The doctrine is, however, based on certain elements taken from Porphyry and Iamblichus, although neither of these affirms that demons are souls of deceased men (cf. however, Proclus, in *Tim.* 24, D, where he reports that Porphyry distinguished three classes of demons, one of which is the pre-existing souls of human beings).   Plotinus affirms (*Enn.* III, 4, 6; III, 5, 6) that demons are wicked, stupid, and have bodies of fire and air; Iamblichus holds (*De. Myst.* II, 6) that the demons are irrational and cannot be free from sense-perception. Both Porphyry and Iamblichus insist on distinguishing between good and bad demons; according to Porphyry (*De Abst.* II, 38 sq.; Procl. op. cit, 53A, 54A) good demons rule matter, while the bad ones are ruled by matter assigned to them and they also change their forms (*De Abst.* II, 37, etc.)—indeed, according to Porphyry (Sent. 32) even the human souls, when they leave their body in an aery encasement (pneuma) can change forms according as they are influenced by their imagination.

79. It is interesting to note that certain contemporary philosophers have also tried to explain abnormal mental phenomena on lines resembling these, cf., e.g. C. D. Broad (*The Mind and its place in Nature*, p. 540), seeking to explain certain abnormal phenomena of knowledge through mediums, 'Now . . . we can suppose that the psychic factor may persist for a time at least after the destruction of the organism with which it was united to form the compound called 'John Jones's mind.' This psychic factor is not itself a mind, but it may carry modifications due to ex-periences which happened to John Jones while he was alive. And it may become temporarily united with the organism of an entranced medium.'

It emerges here (although, as we saw previously, Avicenna rejects any kind of bodily survival, even in the form of a pneumatic body) that at least in the case of some undeveloped souls there must be a kind of bodily survival so that they can have sense-perception.

80. *Najāt*, pp. 303, 18–304, 9; also *Ishārāt* III, pp. 226–7. It is perhaps interesting that al-Fārābī, who in his *Madīna*, p. 53, also starts by des-cribing the social nature of man, proceeds directly to describe what a good or ideal state is and does not refer to the essentially egoistic genesis of morality 'by convention'. Al-Fārābī, who has written much on the state, seems to me more of an idealist and his constructions of the good and the bad states are rather theoretical extremes, although as we shall see later, this idealism does not prevent him from laying down pragmatic criteria for the recognition of the true law-giver.

The idea of man as social animal is of course based on Plato and Aristotle who say that social life is the peculiarity of man alone; only God or animals can do without it. The doctrine that man's nature is essentially egoistic and it is only perforce that he recognizes others' rights against him—the contractual theory put forward in modern times by Hobbes, is expounded and defended in Plato's *Republic* by a character called Glaucon.

The specifically religious turn which the Muslim philosophers give to the doctrine in making the function of law-giving that of a prophet is later Greek. The Greeks, when they began to explain rationally and 'historically' the popular cults of leaders, statesmen, law-givers and inventors of cultural amenities, developed the doctrine of a three-fold theology. Most probably the originator of this doctrine was the Stoic Panätius. One of these, the *theologia civilis*, is explained in a well-known passage of Polybius (VI, 56): 'If one could build a state of wise men, all this would be unnecessary. Since, however, the masses are thoughtless and full of impulses contrary to law, of irrational anger and aggressive in-clinations, nothing else remains but that they should be controlled through the fear of the Unseen. Hence, it seems to me, the Ancients have, with good thought and not purposelessly and haphazardly, introduced into the masses the ideas about gods and belief in the Hades. . . .' It will also be noticed that the account given in this passage of the origin of morality and law is the same as that of Avicenna.

81. Al-Fārābī, *Taḥṣil-al-Saʿāda*, pp. 41, 12–42, 3; also ibid. *Siyāsāt*, p. 49; *Madīna*. p. 57, 16 sq.; Avicenna, *Najāt*, p. 304, 19, 'When such a man does exist, it is necessary that he should promulgate law among people by the command and permission of God, through His revelation and His sending down upon him the Holy Spirit.'

82. Al-Fārābī, *Siyāsāt*, pp. 50, 20–51, 5; see also *Madīna*, p. 60.

83. Avicenna, *Najāt*, pp. 305, 22–306, 10. Avicenna then proceeds to describe the philosophy behind the several religious institutions of Islam, including Jihād.

84. In n. 80.

85. See further on the cultural aspect, Chapter III, section on Ibn Ḥazm's foundation of the doctrine of prophecy on cultural inventions.

86. It should be noted that these three forms broadly correspond to the three aspects of the Muslim philosophers' conception of prophecy: the philosophical with the intellectual revelation; the 'mythical' with the 'imaginative' revelation, and the legal (civilis) with the Sharīʿa. That modifications of detail (e.g. in the place of pagan gods appear angels, etc.) should have occurred is understandable and was, indeed, inevitable. Understandable again, and, indeed, natural is the fact that the attitude of Jewish, Christian and Muslim allegorist philosophers to their traditional religions is certainly not as radical and severe as that of the Greek

rationalists to *their* popular religion (a fact on which H. A. Wolfson seeks to build so much of Philo's originality). For the pagan popular religion, as compared to these three religions was, after all, a crude network of mythology.

87. The Muslim philosophers do not explicitly distinguish between national or local religions and universal religions. They do not, therefore, contrast, from this point of view, e.g. Judaism and Islam. For them, a religious system would have the best claims for universality, which uses a symbolism as near to the higher truth as possible, and such religion for them is, either implicitly or explicitly, Islam.

88. *Najāt*, p. 304.

89. The teaching that there is an inner compulsion in philosophy and wisdom to create a state is not Platonic but Aristotelian. 'A felicitous or virtuous individual man' is, for Aristotle, an imperfect concept, since real moral virtue can be realized only in a community: εἰ γὰρ καὶ ταυτόν ἐστιν (τὸ τελός) ἑνὶ καὶ πόλει, μεῖζόν γε καὶ τελεώτερον τὸ τῆς πόλεως φαίνεται καὶ λαβεῖν καὶ σώζειν· ἀγαπητὸν μὲν γὰρ καὶ ἑνὶ μόνῳ, κάλλιον δὲ καὶ θειότερον ἔθνει καὶ πόλεσιν (*Eth. Nic.* I, 1, 1094b 7). Plato, on the other hand (*Rep.* VII, 519b, sq.) says that philosophers who have caught the vision of the good would prefer to remain in their paradise and would be loath to come down to the 'prisoners of the cave' but would be compelled to do so in the interests of the public weal. But this compulsion is not the inner necessity of their knowledge and wisdom but an external one. I do not, therefore, think A. E. Taylor quite correct when he says, 'The philosopher is the man who has found the way which leads to this beatitude. At the same time, *no man lives to himself, and the man who is advancing to beatitude himself is inevitably animated by the spirit of a missionary to the community at large . . . etc.*' (*Plato, the Man and His Work*, 1926, p. 266.)

90. Plato and Pythagoras came, according to the Muslim philosophers, nearer to their idea than Aristotle for they did not express the bare truth to the public but couched it in symbolic forms: 'It has been said that the prophet must use his words as parables and allusions. . . . And so the Greek philosophers, like Pythagoras, Socrates and Plato, used in their works these forms wherein they entombed their secrets. Plato, indeed, rebuked Aristotle for publicizing the (pure) philosophy, so that Aristotle said that although he had doubtless done this, he had nevertheless left gaps in his works, which only the wise could understand.' (Avicenna, *Tis' Rasā'il*, pp. 124, 23–25, 4).

91. This is a substantially changed version of Plato's *Politicus* (292 E sq.):

'Socrates: . . . For the man who possesses the kingly science, whether he rule or not, must be called kingly. . . .

Stranger: . . . And in agreement with this, we must, I suppose, look for the right kind of rule in one or two or very few men, whenever such right rule occurs. . . . And these men, whether they rule over willing or unwilling subjects, with or without written laws, and whether they are rich or poor, must, according to our present opinion, be supposed to exercise their rule in accordance with some art or science. And physicians offer a particularly good example of this point of view. Whether they cure us against our will or with our will . . . and whether they are rich or poor, we call them physicians just the same, so long as they exercise authority by art or science. . . . It is then a necessary consequence that among forms of government that one is pre-eminently right and is the only real government, in which the rulers are found to be truly possessed of science, not merely to *seem* (δοκοῦντας = ẓannuhum in the above quotation from al-Fārābī) to possess it, whether they rule by law or without law, whether their subjects are willing or unwilling, and whether they themselves are rich or poor—none of these things can be at all taken into account on any right method.' (cf. also the *Republic*, 488b sq. where the 'philosopher's' inability to rule actually is attributed to the obduracy of the people).

Plato goes on to modify this stand in the following and accepts the necessity of law in the absence of the ideal king. The point at issue, however, is that al-Fārābī regards as an essential criterion of true rulership the fact that the ruler *actually succeeds* in obtaining the support and co-operation of people in promulgating his religio-political system at large. This is a quasi-pragmatic criterion, whereas, according to Plato, the real rulership is distinguishable from its 'imitations' only by the possession of the science of state-craft.

Avicenna, too, regards the prophet's success in getting wide acceptance as a matter of central importance and it is in this connection that he invokes his doctrine of miracles: 'It is necessary that the prophet should have a special characteristic distinguishing him from people, who become aware of something in him which they do not possess. Therefore he possesses miracles which we have spoken of' (*Najāt*, p. 304, 17 sq.). Miracles by themselves are not the sufficient cause of his success but only in so far as they can point to the divine mission of the prophet. That is why the last sentence of the *Najāt* says, 'And he is a man who is distinguished from the rest of the people by his divinity (ta'alluh)', and the last sentence of the *Shifā*' even says 'And he is almost worthy of being worshipped.' (There are long discussions in Muslim theology on the evidentiary force of miracles.)

92. The distinction between these two types of knowledge is Platonic-

Aristotelian, but there is an important difference which, as we shall show, pre-supposes later developments in Greco-Roman religious philosophy. Whereas, for Plato and Aristotle, rational knowledge and opinion, conviction and persuasion (or 'imagination') have different *types* of object, for al-Fārābī in this passage they have the *same* objects and are different ways of knowing them.

93. In this passage the word used in the Hydarabad edition for the first four times is *malaka*, but *milla* is used three times after this. *Milla* means a religiously organized community, which is the reading I have adopted here and which squares perfectly with the account of organized state-religion (theologia civilis) of later Greek philosophy; the word *malaka* I cannot understand in this sense.

94. As shown in Section III of this chapter, the Muslim philosophers are against this type of religion since it is not true philosophy but neither does it succeed in inspiring people to goodness which is the essential function of religion.

95. 'Water' is probably an allusion to a Sufic tradition according to which God's throne before creation was on water from which, as material, the world was made.

96. An allusion to the religious account of a material paradise.

97. An allusion to the religious account of temporal creation which the philosophers of Islam deny.

98. Augustine, *De. Civ. Dei.*, IV, 27: Relatum est in litteras, doctissimum pontificem Scaevolam disputasse tria genera tradita deorum; unum a poetis, alterum a philosophis, tertium a principibus civitatis. . . . Secundum (sc. genus) non congruere civitatibus, quod habeat aliqua supervacua, aliqua etiam quae obsit populis nosse. De supervacuis non magna causa est. . . . Quae sunt autem illa quae prolata in multitudinem nocent? Haec, inquit, non esse deos Herculem, Aesculapium . . .; proditur enim a doctis quod homines fuerint et humana conditione defecerint. Quid aliud? Quod earum qui sint dii non habeant civitates (comp. al-Fārābī, above, the underlined words) vera simulacra; quod verus Deus non sexum habeat, nec aetatem, nec definita corporis membra. Haec pontifex . . . expedire existimat, falli in religione civitates.' Augustine adds ironically, 'Praeclara religio, quo confugiat liberandus infirmus, et cum veritatem qua liberetur inquirat, credatur ei expedire quod fallitur!'

The terms of the beliefs in question are, of course, not all identical, but many are parallel.

99. Augustine, op. cit., VI, 5.

100. Al-Fārābī's *sharḥ risāla zainūn al-Kabīr*, Hydarabad, 1349 A.H., p. 9. The treatise has striking similarities with Avicenna rather than with al-Fārābī's doctrine as we know it from his genuine works. See e.g. p. 8: 'The divine prophetic soul in its earliest stage receives the emanation all at once without the need of syllogistic formulation. . . .'

101. ibid., p. 8.

102. P. Gardet, *La Pensée Religieuse d'Avicenne*, p. 203, takes exception to this.

103. ibid, p. 110, last paragraph.

104. This accord is important and, as I have said, explains why the philosophers were not as severe towards orthodoxy as the Stoic philosophers were to their religion. It was, thus, not because of philosophy but of orthodoxy, with the transcendence of God as its central theme, that God did not appear in Islamic culture in the sinewy and finely-chiselled figures as did Apollo and later on Christ. These were the real reasons (and not rhymes and rhythms) for the Koranic rejection of poetry and the 'artistic' religion which is inseparable from all anthropomorphic and polytheistic paganisms.

THREE

THE PHILOSOPHICAL DOCTRINE AND
THE ORTHODOXY

It is not the purpose of this chapter to state in detail the history of the doctrine of prophecy in orthodox Islam, but rather to indicate how the philosophical doctrine was received by it, how far accepted and how far rejected: the discussions of the non-philosophical Muslim thinkers are full of scholastic distinctions and subtleties which the scope of this work does not allow us to indulge in. It is also to be admitted at the outset that it is difficult to define orthodoxy in this field of doctrine. There is first the main body of the scholastic theologians called mutakallimūn who are dogmatic but nevertheless allow the limited use of reason to explain and support the dogma. Then there is the acute form of dogmatism which brushes reason severely aside and uses it only and sometimes very acutely to shatter rationalist positions. Having banished reason altogether, this type of thought, not very common in Islam, seeks support for its dogmatism from the factual experience in history. The former school which is the largest, is admirably represented by al-Shahrastānī, the second by Ibn Ḥazm. In between these two, admitting some kind of 'reason', but rejecting the philosophers altogether, rejecting also Sufism but affirming spiritual values within the framework of Islam, stands the influential figure of Ibn Taymīya who has contributed largely to the resurgence of Islamic anti-classicism and Islamic 'Modernism'. All these schools of thought agree in rejecting the purely intellectualist approach of the philosophers to the phenomenon of prophecy; although the mutakllaimūn are perhaps less averse to accept the intellectual perfection of the prophet, they nevertheless emphasize the Sharī'a-values more than the intellectual ones; and all of them spend most of their ingenuity in discussing the possibility, the nature and the value of miracles.

But these schools do not possess any privileged claim to being exclusively 'orthodox'. There are equally eminent and prominent figures for whom the 'orthodox' community has exceptional reverence[1] and would not allow them to be rejected as 'unorthodox', who have accepted the essentials of the philosophical doctrine *in toto*, and have then tried to weave it into an 'integral Islam'. These are al-Ghazālī and Ibn Khaldūn, the historian. I shall now give a very brief statement of the views of these five authors in chronological order.

1 *Ibn Ḥazm* (d. 456 A.H.)

In the case of Ibn Ḥazm, known as the 'literalist' (al-Ẓāhirī), the possibility of prophecy in both its aspects—supernatural cognition and miracles—depends immediately on his conception of God as being absolute and beyond the categories of human understanding. An omnipotent God who is beyond our moral categories of just and unjust, intentions and purposes and equally beyond our categories of understanding in terms of causation and 'natures' of things, can do anything. In this doctrine our author follows the earlier mutakallimūn who denied causation and 'natures' of things and according to whom God does not do the good and the just but whatever God does is the just and the good. On this principle he denies the view upheld by the Mu'tazila and Avicenna that God *must* send prophets for the guidance of humanity[2]. He thus defines (possible) prophecy as 'sending by God of a group of people (to humanity) whom He has favoured by bestowing excellence upon them—through no other reason but His own will—and to whom He has communicated knowledge without their going through the stages of learning it or their seeking it'.[3]

Prophecy, therefore, is possible. But how do we know that it has actually occurred? Ibn Ḥazm bases his proof on the cultural and scientific development of mankind which could not have come about except through God's communication of knowledge miraculously to a series of prophets (p. 72, 1 sq.):

'We know with certainty that none among us, by dint of his own nature, can discover sciences and arts without being taught, e.g. medicine, the knowledge of natural properties (i.e. the uniform behaviour of natural objects by God's command), of diseases and their various causes and their treatment by herbs which can never be experimented in their totality. . . . Again, e.g. the science of astronomy, how the stars rotate, traverse space and return to their spheres—a performance which takes tens of thousands of years. . . . Or, again, e.g. language without which not only training is impossible but on the whole any activity of life; nor could it have been created

by convention for that already presupposes the use of language'.
Ibn Ḥazm goes on to enumerate other arts like agriculture, weaving,
building and navigation and concludes (72, 16 sq.) 'None of these
can be known without learning. It is then necessarily the case that
there be one or more persons whom God initially taught these things,
without a teacher, through revelation'.[4]

On the same principle of the extreme absolutism of God which
denies real essences or natural powers (since, as creations of God,
they can be changed by him), Ibn Ḥazm grounds the possibility of
miracles (op. cit. p. 73; 17 sq.). His distinction between genuine
miracles and sorcery is made to rest on the doctrine that a sorcerer
can only change (or make believe that he can change) the external,
non essential qualities of things, whereas God, at the hands of a
true prophet, does not only change the essential qualities of things
but can bring new substances into existence (p. 76, 4 sq.) Sorcery
is an art which any man can learn whereas prophecy and miracles
are divinely bestowed.[5] Both, the actuality of the prophet's miracles
and the finality of prophecy with Muḥammad's mission, are based
on the principle of the absolute credibility of an overwhelming,
widespread tradition (pp. 74, 77).
     Ibn Ḥazm's position is that of extreme dogmatism, allowing no
appeal to reason even at a subsidiary level. In so far as he would
not admit any divine purpose (since purpose for him is a purely
human category) in prophetic missions, he is certainly not typical
of Islamic thought on the subject. One cannot speak in his dogmatic
system of any 'de-naturalization' of the phenomenon of prophecy
since he admits no nature. Like Tertullian, he would gladly say
'credo quia absurdum' and like Iamblichus (see above p. 67, 29) he
might well have said that God can create knowledge in a fool.

II Al-Ghazālī (d. 505 A.H.)

Al-Ghazālī is a most difficult author, if not an outright impossible one,
to understand in any coherent manner. This is because in his early
youth he had an acute crisis which destroyed his traditional form of
faith; then in his search for truth he had a series of disillusionments
with various disciplines like Kalām and philosophy culminating
in another crisis until, as he professes in his *Munqidh*, he found
quietude in Sufism. However, although he was dissatisfied with

Kalām and philosophy, both seem to have left indelible influences on him. With Kalām he was dissatisfied, it seems, not because of the metaphysical beliefs which it sought to inculcate but with the purely formal dialectical method it employed. Against philosophers he rose in revolt chiefly because of their theological beliefs to the refutation of which he devoted the greater part of his *Tahāfut*. Nevertheless, in spite of this open revolt, it is impossible to gauge the extent to which he really renounced the doctrines of the philosophers. For, he began to write esoteric treatises in which he admits philosophical doctrines which he rejects in works meant for the public. It is quite clear that these esoteric treatises must have been written after he became fully conscious of the discord between philosophy and Sunni orthodoxy and therefore after his professed 'disillusionment' with philosophy. This is precisely why the establishment of the chronological order of his works (if this could be done) and attempts to lay down criteria for determining his 'genuine' works must fail to clarify his position. In a way, the question about his 'real beliefs' is not a genuine question, for, surely, his genuine beliefs are those contained in the esoteric works? Even the fact that the men who later criticized him from both sides of the fence, all of them accused him of double-mindedness,[6] shows that no criteria, whether gained from the chronology of works or otherwise, are either possible or fruitful.

But even the question of different treatises—esoteric and exoteric —apart, one finds in one and the same work unconcealed contradictions. This can only be because he has sincerely adopted at least some doctrines both from Islamic orthodoxy and from philosophy which are not reconciled but juxtaposed.[7] Under these conditions I propose to give his views on prophecy as he himself has stated them in two different works: the *Ma' ārij-al-Quds* which is professedly esoteric[8] and the *Mi'rāj al-Sālikīn* (Cairo, 1344 A.H.) which is obviously meant for the public and in which he takes the line of the *Tahafūt*.

Al-Ghazālī's account of prophecy in the *Ma' ārij-al-Quds* seems to me to fall into two fairly distinct parts: in the first he gives arguments to establish prophecy and in the second he expounds its working at three levels: of imagination, of intellect and of miracle-performing power. The first part is marked by an attempt to compromise the naturalistic doctrine of philosophy with the supernaturalism of the dogmatic theology; in the second part he borrows entirely and almost literally from Avicenna's account. He offers three arguments for prophecy:—

(1) The first argument seeks to put the class of prophets as a distinct species above man: 'Just as the human species is distinguished from other animals by the rational soul . . . similarly the souls of prophets are distinguished from men's souls by a guiding and guided intellect which is above all (normal) intelligence, rules and governs it through divine excellence. Just as the movements of a human being are miraculous for the rest of animals . . . so are all the movements of a prophet miraculous for human beings' (pp. 144, 15–45, 3). We are also told that 'prophecy is a divine favour and gift which cannot be acquired by effort—although effort and acquisition are necessary to prepare the soul for the reception of revelation by acts of worship accompanied by exercise in thinking and by pure and sincere deeds. Thus prophecy is neither a pure chance (without a natural desert) so that every creeping shuffling creature may be its recipient, nor is it attained by pure effort so that everyone who thinks may have it. . . . Just as humanity is not acquired by individual humans nor angelness by members of the "species" 'angel', but their actions which flow from their specific natures will depend on their effort and choice . . . so prophecy which is the specific nature of the prophets is not acquired by them but their actions which flow from their specific form depend on their acquisition and choice in order to prepare themselves for revelation' (pp. 142, 18–143, 12). Al-Ghazālī then goes on to portray the sound constitution and excellent natural moral character of such a being.

What does this passage seek to perform? It obviously attempts to 'de-naturalize' prophecy, so that not every philosopher or mystic may become a prophet, by positing a species of prophets. But once this species has been posited, prophecy becomes as necessary and 'natural' for each of its members as humanity for a human. The 'divine favour and gift' turns out to be ultimately nothing but certain prophetic capacities which must be realized. Nor had the philosophers said that any human can be a prophet, even though he be a philosopher or a mystic. Far from this, they say that the prophet's soul is endowed with certain intellectual, imaginative and telekinetic capacities which cannot be acquired either by learning or mystic purification.

Al-Ghazālī calls this argument the 'general argument' for the establishment of prophecy: it depends on the positing of a prophetic intellectual power formally and specifically different from ordinary thought.[9] What reasons are there to believe that such a species is actual and, indeed, necessary? To prove this al-Ghazālī offers two arguments, the one starting from man, the other starting from God.

(2) The argument which takes its point of departure from man is, again, twofold, the one strictly moral, the other based on 'utilitarian' or 'conventional' morality. The moral argument runs as follows: The acts which man can perform contain both good and bad ones. Some acts, therefore, must be performed others must be avoided. Not everybody knows where the good ends and the bad begins. *Nevertheless, there must be some who do know these limits (ḥudūd).* These are the prophets, the promulgators of religious laws. As for the *argumentum ab utili*, it is the same as that of Avicenna (see Chap. II, section IV): a legislator is required to determine the rights and duties of individuals *vis-à-vis* one another in a society necessarily dependent on co-operation but wherein individuals are apt to regard self-interest as the only intrinsic governing principle.

Where al-Ghazālī again differs from the philosophers is in his religious impulse which leads him to regard the angels of revelation not as quasi autonomous beings, as the philosophers do, but as beings under the direct order of God to communicate revelation to the prophet: The formulation of the Sharīʿa is not possible 'except if there be a (prophetic) intellect assisted by revelation, destined to prophecy, and drawing help from spiritual beings (angels) which are determined (by God) to preserve the World-order, act according to His Command, conduct themselves *vis-à-vis* His Creation according to his pattern of behaviour, and rule according to His judgment. The commands regarding the law-determinations come to them from God and from them to the person charged with the trust (i.e. the prophet)'[10]—pp. 147, 18–48, 4.

(3) This line of thought leads al-Ghazālī to his third argument which he declares to be the basic one. This seeks to show God to be the First and, indeed, the sole Commander. Everything that moves has a mover; differences in 'natural' movement mean that the mover has will, and, finally, if the movements are for the good, the mover is a Commander. This Command, when necessarily obeyed, as it is by the heavens, is the Command of regimentation or management (ʾamr al-tadbīr), but when faced with a being capable of disobedience as man—who stands at the threshold of good and evil—it is a moral Command (ʾamr-al-taklīf). It follows that there must

D

be human media of transmitting God's Command to humanity. Those who accept God only as creator, deny Him Commands which they attribute 'only to the claimer of prophecy as their sole author, not going beyond him (to God). Thus (according to these people— doubtlessly the philosophers are meant) whenever the prophet says 'God says', 'God admonishes', 'God commands and forbids', 'God promises and threatens', these are a metaphorical mode of speech not a literal one' (p. 151, 4–8). This argument implies, I think, that the souls of the heavenly bodies, the intellects or the angels do not know anything automatically or 'naturally' except what God makes known to them, although al-Ghazālī does not say this expressly here as he does in the 16th Discussion in the *Tahāfut*. The upshot of all this is that al-Ghazālī substitutes God, the Commander, for the Prime Mover and the First of Aristotle and the Muslim Philosophers.

It is obvious that in the foregoing al-Ghazālī takes orthodox Islam as his guiding impulse, and is using philosophy to formulate that Islam.[11] But then follows the chapter on 'the characteristics of prophecy', which is almost word for word borrowed from Avicenna. I need not go into the details of this chapter, since we have previously learnt Avicenna's views. All the three performances of prophecy—intellectual, imaginative and the working of miracles, are attributed to the faculties of the human soul, and we travel far indeed from the conception of God the Commander.

As for the exoteric work, *Miʿrāj al-Sālikīn*, it naturally represents the official, public attitude of al-Ghazālī. The work,[12] divided into seven sections, shows the same indictment of the philosophers as the *Tahāfut* and could be aptly described as the miniature *Tahāfut*. On the subject of prophecy it is more severe towards the philosophers than the *Tahāfut* where, although al-Ghazālī criticizes them, he does not accuse them of *kufr* (rejection of Islam). In the preface to this work, however (p. 8) he says, 'The sixth sect (of Muslims) represents people who have added to it (i.e. to the Muʿtazilite doctrine of God) something on account of which rejection of Islam is attributed to them, e.g. those philosophers who have affirmed prophecy but have interpreted it in the sense of political rule and have believed that at his very birth the prophet (has certain dispositions which) render him capable of political control, that he possesses (natural excellence) and is, therefore, followed by people. These people are outside Islam'.

In the 5th Section, again, devoted to prophecy (p. 73) he says that of those who affirm prophecy one party 'asserts that it is some-thing necessitated by the person's (dispositions acquired at) birth so that his soul is possessed of a faculty which can cause changes in nature and renders him of excellent character and conduct. This is the philosophers' doctrine'. Al-Ghazālī then goes on to give an account of prophecy in accordance with the official Kalām, but (p. 74, 9–10) denies that politico-legal management (siyāsa) is a part of prophecy. This denial does not belong to Kalām and is most probably to be traced to the author's mysticism. Nevertheless, in connection with proving the prophetic mission of Muḥammad in the same section (p. 75, 1–2) he points to the political management of people (siyāsat al-khalq) through the Sharī'a law.

Despite this 'super-naturalism', however, al-Ghazālī admits natural degrees of human capacity to receive revelation and the intellectual nature of the angels: 'But for the intelligences known as angels which help the souls from outside these latter would not understand anything. For the (human) soul which is only potentially cognizant is rendered actually so by the angels' actualization of its potentialities. The highest rank in securing this help are the prophets. . . . The humans differ in their acquisition of knowledge from the angel, a difference which admits of infinite grades' (p. 32, 8–16). The most vivid impression emerging from these two state-ments is that certain orthodox beliefs and certain philosophical doctrines remained permanent elements of al-Ghazālī's mind, some-times in blatant contradiction; the one side may gain prominence over the other according to the people he was addressing and the other may get modified, and that neither had he ever embraced the whole of philosophy and given up orthodox beliefs even before his 'return', nor after his 'return', did he ever give up certain philo-sophical tenets even if they contradicted the orthodox position. The nearest he comes to reconciling the two is in the first part of his teaching on Prophecy in the Ma'ārij al-Quds.

III Kalām—al-Shahrastānī (d. 548 A.H.)

The greatest emphasis in the Kalām-doctrine of prophecy is that it is a special divine favour by virtue of which the recipient of the prophetic mission is singled out from the rest of mankind. In this doctrine, therefore, miracles occupy the most prominent place,

since the appointment of an individual to the office is itself miraculous. The general possibility of prophecy is sought to prove
rationally by the same argument about the necessity of establishing
social order which was used by Avicenna and Al-Ghazālī.[13] But
the actual appointment of a definite individual to the office rests
on divine grace and favour.

According to al-Shahrastānī, the prophet must, indeed, possess
all the 'natural' qualities (including the intellectual ones), to the
highest degree and he may even be said to attain prophecy by virtue
of these qualities: 'By my life! the prophet's soul and temperament
must possess all natural perfection, excellent character, truthful-
ness and honesty in speech and deed before his appointment to the
office because it is *by virtue of* these that he has deserved prophetic
mission and has come into contact with angels and received revelation.'[14] But still we may not say that he himself, by these qualities,
has *achieved* prophecy: 'Those who are on the right say that prophecy
is not a quality referable to the soul of the prophet, nor is it a
status to which anyone can reach through his knowledge and acquisition or capacity of his soul by virtue of which he deserved a
contact with the spiritual realm. It is a mercy and grace of God.'[15]

This apparent contradiction in a single passage is to be solved
by pointing out that the possession by the prophet of these qualities
itself represents the grace of God: 'When God singles some one out
for the prophetic office from among His servants, He decorates
him with the robe of beauty in his words, morals and his (spiritual
and physical) states, so that the whole creation cannot counter him
with any of these things. Then all his movements become miraculous
for other people, just as the movements of the humans are miraculous
for the lower animals (comp. al-Ghazālī, above p. 96). He is thus
able to subdue the human race (to his obedience), just as man is
able to subdue other species of animal.'[16]

The prophet is a human but a special kind of human: 'They have
two sides: human and prophetic (as the Koran says) 'Say: glory be to
God, am I but a human being and a prophet?' So, on the side of
humanness the prophet partakes of the human species: he eats and
drinks, sleeps and wakes, lives and dies, while on the side of prophecy
he partakes of the species of angels: he glorifies God and sanctifies
His transcendence, lives in Him and is fed by Him; his eyes sleep
but not his heart. . . .'[17] This passage, which identifies a prophet
qua prophet with the angel (or, in philosophical terminology, with

the Active Intelligence) is very strikingly close to the philosophical view of the relationship between the prophet and the angel. Yet, the two have different reasons. Whereas, the philosophers are led to this view by their theory of knowledge, the identity of the subject and the object etc., the theologian is forced by the doctrine of the miraculousness of prophecy and the impeccability of the prophet. Most later Kalām-theologians, however, do not affirm this identity and regard the quality of prophecy as a purely human attribute. Al-Shahrastānī here clearly shows, I think, the influence of Avicenna and al-Ghazālī.[18]

<h2 style="text-align:center">iv Ibn Taymīya (d. 728 A.H.)</h2>

Ibn Taymīya wrote a special book on Prophecy (*K. al-Nubuwwāt*, Cairo, 1346 A.H.). His formal doctrine, characterized again by a prominence of the discussion of miracles, does not differ from that of the general Kalām, except on minor points of detail, and I should not have deemed it as such worthy of a special attention. But what makes it both interesting and unique is his setting of the problem of prophecy in his *Weltanschauung* and his severe critique of the philosophers' theory which follows from this general setting. In doing so, Ibn Taymīya, so far as I know, is the only medieval Muslim who seeks to formulate clearly the ultimate issues at stake between the cognitive approach to reality of the Greeks and the 'anti-classical' attitudes of the Koran.

According to Ibn Taymīya, the goal of human life is neither the philosophic contemplation of God nor the mystic type of love of Him —for each of these leads to the doctrine of the Unity of Being, of the identity of the world and God and so to the absolute inanity both of God and man—but the active concept of '*ibāda*, a knowledge of God's will and its fearless implementation in life. God is not something to be merely perceived, or admired and cherished but must be recognized as the One to whom alone our allegiance is due. This recognition alone is describable as *Tauḥīd* (monotheism) and it alone can inspire the attitude of '*ibāda* (*al-Nubuwwāt*, pp. 77–79,6). Ibn Taymīya is then ready to lash his attack against philosophy and Sufism.

'According to the so-called philosophers there are three kinds of happiness, sensual, imaginative and intellectual which is knowledge. . . . Thus they came to regard knowledge itself as the goal of human life . . . and hold that the happiness of the soul consists in

D:

the knowledge of eternal things because it acquires eternity itself thanks to the eternity of the object of knowledge. Then they imagine that the heavens, their souls and the intelligences are indestructible and that the soul acquires happiness through knowing them.

'Abū Ḥāmid (al-Ghazālī), in his works like the *Miʿrāj al-Sālikīn*, also suggests this. His statements are a bridge between the Muslims and the philosophers. . . . This is why in his works like the *Iḥyāʾ* he teaches that the goal of all action is only knowledge, which is also the essence of the philosophers' teaching. He magnifies the renunciation of the world which was his greater pre-occupation than *Tauḥīd* which is the *ʿibāda* of God alone. *Tauḥīd* alone comprises also the true love of God. . . .

'These so-called philosophers magnify the separation of the soul from the material body, which means renuciation of the physical desires and of the world. But this only leads to a vacuity of the soul which vacuity is then dressed up by the devil in the garb of intuitive experience of which the end is absolute and abstract being (i.e. Unity of all being) which has no existence in the real world.

'In pursuance of this Abū Ḥāmid has divided the mystic path into three stages. . . . (p. 80, 18) His statements of this kind are frequent and they terrify one who does not understand his real purpose, since their author knows fully well and intimately what he is talking about and does not speak on the blind-following of another authority alone. The question, however, is whether what he says is right . . . (p. 81, 1). What he has made the goal of human life, viz. the *knowledge* of God, His attributes, His actions, and of angels, in his *al-Maḍnūn*—which is pure philosophy—is worse than the beliefs of the idolatrous Arabs, let alone of Jews and Christians.' (pp. 79, 6–81, 2).

Ibn Taymīya then goes on to affirm that the purpose of man is not mere knowledge of God but his *ʿibāda* i.e. to recognize that allegiance is due only to God and actively to implement it in life, to reject all other authority, natural or supernatural, as pure sham. One sees at once the animating force lying behind this attack: that crusading moral imperative which first seeks to crush out of its way the drugs of superstition and then impel to action to restore moral order in individual and social life. In both these aspects, this activism of Ibn Taymīya has throbbed in the veins of Modern Islam as a whole.

The revelation of the divine wisdom and will must emanate from God Himself and must in no sense depend on the natural operation of the human mind itself. The basic heresy of the philosophers lies in the fact that they have not done justice to the true majesty of God and His revelation. True, they have affirmed that the author of revelation is the Active Intelligence, but still their essential doctrine remains humanistic:

'The furthest removed from (a genuine conception of) prophecy are the so-called philosophers, the Baṭinīs (esoterists) and the extravagant heretics (malāḥida). These people recognize prophecy to be only something commonly shared by all human beings, e.g. dreams. In Aristotle and his followers there is no mention of the prophetic revelation. Al-Fārābī makes it only of the order of dreams and that is why he and others like him affirm the superority of the philosopher over the prophet.

'Avicenna has done it more honour than this and has posited three characteristics of the prophet: first, that the prophet obtains knowledge without being taught. This—the power of intuition—he calls the Holy faculty. Secondly, the prophet's imagination symbolizes this intellectual knowledge and thus he sees in his own soul psychic (rūḥānī) forms and also hears in his own mind voices . . . but so does the melancholic according to them. Thirdly, the prophet has a mental power whereby he can influence the matter of the world, and produce strange events which they regard as miracles. . . .

'These people do not admit that transcending the highest sphere there may be something which can act or produce. So there is nothing beyond which speaks or moves in any way—not even an angel let alone the Lord of the World. These people also affirm intelligences which do not change and move, have no speech and have no action, and so their first principle. According to them whatever comes to the mind of the prophets comes from the Active Intelligence.

'But when they heard of the prophets' revelations, they wanted to reconcile this phenomenon with their doctrines. They took the teminology of the prophets and denoted by them their own concepts . . . and so people who do not know the meaning of the prophets think that both parties are talking of the same thing.' (ibid. p. 168, 4–23).

After accusing al-Ghazālī of oscillation between philosophy and

Islam and saying that whereas in his *Tahāfut*, he accuses the philosophers of infidelity, he follows them completely elsewhere in his
discussions of prophecy, Ibn Taymīya, goes on (p. 169, 14 sq.):

'According to them, what the prophet possesses of intuition and
verbal revelation is of the same kind as that which magicians and
demented fools have, the only difference being that the one commands good while the other commands evil and the demented have
no intelligence. This amount of difference exists even among ordinary people and thus the prophet has no essential distinction from
the magician and the demented . . . (line 23). This is a master-
piece of Avicenna's sagacity. When he was informed of strange
phenomena in the world (like prophecy and magic) which he could
not deny, he attempted to interpret them on philosophical principles
as he says expressly in his *Ishārāt*.'

Ibn Taymīya holds that neither sorcery and soothsaying depend
on the power of the soul nor the prophetic revelation: the former
depends on evil spirits and devils, the other on God and the angels.
'The philosophers have, therefore, not given to prophecy its due
place and thus many so-called Sufis . . . like Ibn 'Arabī and Ibn
Sab'īn have been misled by them, who accepted this philosophical
theory and operated upon it with their own mysticism. That is why
Ibn 'Arabī says that saints are better than prophets' (p. 172, 12–15).
This is because Ibn 'Arabī thought that he had direct access to the
intellectual source of which the angel which inspires the prophet
is only a symbol created by the imaginative faculty.
    The author then defines (p. 172, 23) a prophet (Nabī) as a man
whom God sends a message. The ordinary prophet is a reformer: he
brings a message to a people who do not contest the truth of the
message but are simply morally not living up to what they recognize
as true. The prophet's function is to reform them morally. But
when a people refuses to accept the very truth, the task of the
prophet is of a revolutionary character. His function is that of a
socio-moral crusader (like Moses and Muḥammad) and very often
such a kind of prophet (called Rasūl) brings with him a new Sharī'a
—a socio-moral code to establish a new order of society (p. 173).
    In passages like those quoted above Ibn Taymīya breaks through
the scholastic formalism of the Kalām and grapples with what are the
basic issues between the intellectualist ethics of Hellenism and the

moral dynamism of the Semitic tradition. He rejects the concept of the purely cognitive goal of human life because he thinks that, despite the efforts of the Muslim philosophers to safeguard the transcendence of God and of truth, the intellectual approach to reality is essentially humanist and destroys the absolute character of the moral imperative. It is to be noted that his reaction is not only against philosophy but is even more severely directed against mysticism. He wishes to destroy the intellectualism of Avicenna because it has prepared the way for Ibn 'Arabī's doctrine of the Unity of Being (Waḥdat-al-wujūd).

v *Ibn Khaldūn* (d. 808 A.H.)

Ibn Khaldūn's views, in the last section of the first chapter of his *Muqaddima*, are very interesting and his discussion of the different known types of occult knowledge is full of subtle distinctions. But his views on the subject have not been studied so far. His account of prophecy seeks to reconcile the orthodox and the rationalists' claims and attempts to rationalize the supernaturalism of the orthodox kalām.

According to Ibn Khaldūn, the whole created nature represents a system or structure composed of hierarchic grades or levels. Each level has two limits (ufuq) whereby it is distinguished from the immediately lower and superior levels. The levels are not, however, absolutely closed from one another but have intermediate links (ittiṣāl). Thus there are certain things which are neither pure minerals nor pure plants and similarly there are things, like the jelly-fish, which are both plants and animals. The levels run into one another and, Ibn-Khaldūn asserts, at these limits, it is possible that certain members of one species progress to the higher species or devolve to the lower species. 'The meaning of the linkage . . . is that the upper end of a certain level has a perfected capacity (*al-istiʿdād al-qarīb*, as opposed to the "remote capacity") or absolute preparedness to become the first part of the higher level'.[19] This assertion is not made in connection with any doctrine of evolution but to explain the known facts in the fields of rational and social sciences and religion.

Man's analysis reveals a double nature: corporeal and spiritual. By virtue of his spiritual nature man stands at the threshold of, and some rare men can, through their endowment of immense spiritual power, enter into, the sublime angelic realm: 'This argument necessitates that (some human) souls have a (perfected) capacity to jump out of (insilākh or inqilāʿ) humanness into angelicness and actually become of the species of angels at some moment of time after the perfection of their own spiritual character. . . . In its linkage, therefore, the soul has an upper side and a lower side; by its lower side it is linked to the body whereby it acquires sense-knowledge which gives it the capacity to acquire actual intellection, while on its upper end it is linked with the angelic level whereby it acquires (higher) knowledge of the Unseen'.[20]

Ibn Khaldūn then proceeds to describe three types of human souls. The first is dependent in its cognitive functions entirely on psycho-physical functions of sense-perception, imagination and memory. These people can 'only combine concepts (acquired through sense-perception) according to certain definite and limited (logical) laws.' The movement of their thought is dependent on the body and thus limited. These, the common run of scholars and thinkers, are, therefore essentially unoriginal. The second class of men turn the movement of their thought away from the closed circle of primary and self-evident (al-awwalīyāt) truths to purely spiritual knowledge, since their mental and spiritual powers are greater. These men, being original thinkers, not only reason by the combinations of concepts and judgments, but directly intuite, and, not being fettered by the necessarily limited range of the first category, have unlimited scope of knowledge. These are people of genuine mystic experience.

But whereas even the second category moves only within the confines of the human soul itself, although touching its highest and purely spiritual limits, it is only in the case of the prophet that the human soul is transformed into a higher, angelic selfhood, as we have learnt before. While the perfection attained by the mystic in this life may be attained by many good souls in the life beyond, the prophetic perfection is limited to the prophets, not attainable by any effort or acquisition.[21] Again, the prophetic revelation is of two types. Either the prophet hears a kind of inarticulate internal sound, or he visibly perceives the angel. In both cases, the message having been received, the prophet 'returns' to the human self and the message transforms itself in terms of human understanding, so that humanity at large may be able to understand it. But whereas in the first case the prophet's understanding of the revelation is not concurrent with the revelatory process, but suddenly dawns upon him at the end (perhaps the prophet's interpretation is involved in this) and, further, it invariably takes the form of speech at the human level, the second form of revelation is clearer, is simultaneously understood and hence the prophet *sees* the angel, since sight is the clearest of all senses.[22]

It is obvious that Ibn Khaldūn has devised this scheme in order to meet the requirements both of philosophy and of orthodox Kalām, represented, e.g. by al-Shahrastānī. He admits certain natural capacities (on the basis of which he also establishes the doctrine of 'iṣma or impeccability of the prophets) by which the prophet is able to identify himself with a subliminal self, and yet he moves strictly within the formal distinctions of the orthodox theology. Actually, the doctrine is fundamentally the same as that of the philosophers; only these had not expressed their distinctions formally, and, indeed, on the subject of miracles they found themselves unable to make any distinction. But on this subject Ibn Khaldūn is able to make a distinction only by adopting the Kalām-doctrine *in toto* and by giving up all talk of natural faculties of the soul.

The one striking point on which Ibn Khaldūn differs from the philosophers and the one crucial point in the philosophical doctrine perhaps most repugnant to orthodoxy concerns the actual verbal revelation and the whole status of the Sharī'a. The philosophers had held that these are not the pure truth but were symbolic representations of it, created by the strong imaginative power of the prophet. For Ibn Khaldūn, the actual recorded revelation—the Koran—is certainly the human form of the purely spiritual divine 'logos', but there is no suggestion that it is only symbolic. He does not allow even a psychological gap between the word and the spiritual message so that the former might be regarded as an interpretation by the prophet himself of the latter, at least in the second of the two types of prophetic revelation noted above.

The subject of imagination is introduced in a different context, viz. in order to explain dreams but mostly to explain certain other occult forms of cognition, like soothsaying (kahāna). Soothsayers, diviners and magicians, we are told (p. 84, 14 sq.) also depend for their performance on the natural faculties of their souls. But neither are they able to transform (insilākh) their souls into subliminal selves like the prophets, nor, indeed, are their souls strong enough for mystical achievements. They are weaklings with an ambition to become prophet-like. Since they have not much natural capacity, they take recourse to employing the aid of extraneous elements, like mirrors, the hearts of animals etc., to derive inspiration. When they do get inspiration, these external images, which have already become firmly fixed in their strong imaginative faculty, become mixed up with it and interfere. That is why in their reports truth and falsehood are mixed:—

'Since the division of men has shown us that there exists another type of man whose intellective faculty is impelled by nature to move deliberately (towards transforming itself into a higher self) and that by its nature also falls short of this, it tends to recline upon individual objects sensible or imaginary—like translucent bodies, the bones of animals, rhymed prose or what appears suddenly to vision of birds or animals. It then seeks to retain (in its mental concentration) this sensation or image trying to take help from it in its endeavour to transform itself. It is this faculty in them which is the source of their soothsaying cognition. Since such souls are by nature imperfect, their cognition of individuals is stronger than that of universals, and that is why their imaginative faculty is extremely strong because imagination is the instrument of apprehending individuals.' (p. 84, 23–85, 2). (p. 85, 6) 'So by the co-operation of (his natural mental) movement and this extraneous element, certain occurrences take place in his mind which he ejects through his tongue. He is sometimes right and sometimes false—in fact, mostly false because his natural imperfection is completed only by the aid of an external factor'. It is obvious that on the same grounds Ibn Khaldūn would reject as fakes experiments of modern students of religious psychology by the introduction of drugs and hypnosis. Indeed (p. 93) he also condemns the practices of certain *yogis* who seek to contact the Unseen by mortification of physical faculties. Apart from the fact that no adequate knowledge of the Unseen can be gained in this manner, he finds their aims morally indictable. One's aim should be devotion to God and not the gaining of occult knowledge. Islamic orthodoxy had, of course, always regarded these procedures of obtaining knowledge as highly dubious and mostly even outright condemnable.

CONCLUDING REMARKS

After winding one's way through long and intricate, and often dismally formal discussions of our subject across the centuries, one may wonder if there is any basic difference between the philosophical and non-philosophical positions. At first sight it appears that orthodoxy would be satisfied if the direct divine authorship of miracles is affirmed instead of referring these to the natural capacities of the human soul as the philosophers had done, and if the philosophical dictum that the Revelation and the Shari'a are only symbolic expressions of a higher truth is rejected or drastically modified. For, leaving miracles aside, and taking the basic manner and form of Revelation itself, there would hardly seem to be any difference. According to the philosophers, the prophet receives Revelation by identifying himself with the Active Intellect; according to al-Shahrastānī, an eminent representative of the Kalām, and Ibn Khaldūn, by no means a heretic, the prophet is identified with the angel (although many rightists like Ibn Taymīya would deny this identification, saying that it is impossible for a human to transcend humanity at any point or in any way, even if he receives suprahuman knowledge). Again, the outward anxiety of the orthodoxy appears to be that the philosophers' doctrine would tend to make prophets of men rather easily since their talk of the natural capacities of the human soul does not allow of any limit where ordinary humanity stops and prophecy begins. And thus orthodoxy comes to formulate its anxiety in terms of naturalism and non-naturalism, i.e. divine grace and favour. But al-Shahrastānī, as we saw above, sees this divine grace itself, despite certain statements to the contrary, expressed in the natural capacities of the prophet to contact the angel or be identified with it, and Ibn Khaldūn clearly speaks of the natural powers of the human soul. On the other hand, the philosophers themselves categorically deny that any and every thinker or mystic could be a prophet and indeed as our analysis showed, they had in their mind certain fixed images, of Muḥammad *par excellence*. One cannot, therefore, help thinking that the formal issue of naturalism and non-naturalism is a symptom of something deeper.

The fundamental gap, as we pointed out while discussing al-Ghazālī and Ibn Taymīya, between the orthodox and the philosophical *weltanschauung*, concerns the nature of man and therefore of the nature of the divine message to the prophet. According to the philosophers the goal of man in which his ultimate bliss consists is the· contemplation of reality; in their thoroughly intellectualist-mystical attitude to life, life of religio-moral action is at best a ladder which is to be transcended. The orthodox impulse is activist; it does not reject intellectualism but subordinates it to the end of moral dynamism. The philosophers' reality is an immobile eternal truth; the orthodoxy's ultimate reality is also certain eternal truth, but being primarily a moral truth, it must result in moral action. The orthodox conception of truth is therefore not of something which merely *is* but essentially of something which 'commands'. It is thus the evaluation of the Sharī'a that is at stake. This issue is implicit in the orthodox Kalām, but is explicitly formulated by Ibn Taymīya and partly by al-Ghazālī.

Further, the orthodox feel that the true imperativeness of this moral truth cannot be sufficiently guarded unless it is posited above humanity as such. And here we see the very different motives which have led both the philosophers and some of the orthodox to the apparently identical dictum, viz. that the prophet is identical with the angel. The orthodox feel that the philosophers have brought the angel down to man; their own solution is to raise man, in certain defined cases, up to the angel. It is this motive, and not the philosophical principle of the theory of knowledge concerning the identity of the intellect and the intelligible, that has led some of the orthodox to this identification dictum. Again, according to the philosophers, despite their—and especially Avicenna's—efforts to safeguard the 'separateness' of the Active Intelligence, the *raison d'être* of the latter is really the intellectual guidance of humanity: its very epithet 'Active' shows that its central—if indeed not its entire—function is to create forms in nature and especially in man. And for Averroes, the eternal existence of the Universal Intellect and of thinking humanity are co-relates, as it were.[23] This quasi-immanentism and humanism perhaps seemed to orthodox Islam even more dangerous than the temporary identity of the prophet with the divine in the act of revelation. For, even though the involvement of the divine in the creation and especially in man is great and, indeed, crucial for man's fate, to exhaust the meaning of the divine—the transcendant eternal truth—in man's destiny is even far more intolerable than the emptying of man's being in the divine.

NOTES

1. One would not be wrong, I think, in saying that the influence of al-Ghazālī and Ibn Taymīya, taken singly, on the Muslim community as a whole, has been greater than that of the totality of scholastic theologians. Paradoxical though it may seem, the community's concrete attitudes have not regarded spiritualization and fundamentalism as incompatibles, although extremists like the Wahhābīs and extreme Sufis have done so.

2. *Kitāb al-Fiṣal fi'l-milal wa'l-ahwā' wa'l-niḥal* (Cairo, 1317 A.H.) p. 69.

3. ibid., p. 71, 20–22.

4. This argument is not altogether different from that of Avicenna (*Najāt, Psychology*, Ch. 6) where he argues that each science has certain ultimate and basic premises (an Aristotelian doctrine) and that these must have been discovered by prophets by intuition. But whereas Avicennian intuition is a 'natural' occurrence, Ibn Ḥazm's revelation is miraculous—indeed, there can be nothing 'natural' in Ibn Ḥazm's view.

Al-Ghazālī also employed this argument from the scientific cultural development (in his *Munqidh*) which Ibn Taymīya rejects saying (*K. al-Nubuwwāt*, p. 22) that to reason to the existence of prophecy from the existence of sciences is like reasoning to the existence of medicine from that of poetry, indeed, even more fantastic.

The idea of the divine origin of the development of human culture is rooted in Greek antiquity. The Greeks were very fond of collecting the inventors or supposed inventors of cultural amenities, the πρῶτοι εὑρεται (the oldest of the extant lists is in *Pliny, N.H.*, VII, 191 sq.). In Greek mythology these arts—and later on in Prodicus—also the inventors of these arts are deified (see Prodicus, fragment 5, in Diels), as heroes and gods. Prometheus and Palamedes, Demeter and Dionysus are celebrated and honoured as discoverers of agriculture, etc. In Euripides (*Hik.*, V, 201 sq.) not only are intelligence and speech endowed by a god but also agriculture, clothing, navigation and the art of soothsaying are taught to man by him. The catalogue of cultural discoveries includes, of course, also the institution of religion and state. But as the Euhemeristic and philosophical interpretations of the origin of mythology developed, these heroes and gods were rewritten as the wise men of the pre-historic past as we find in the philosopher-poet Critias and in Stoics like Poseidonius. In Muslim popular belief the Judaeo-Koranic prophets were hailed as cultural benefactors of mankind.

5. This distinction is a changed version of the distinction (see above, p. 66) between the 'natural' and 'cultivated' forms of prophecy. The 'natural' form here appears—as in Christian accounts—as the direct work of God.

6. Ibn Taymīya, op. cit., p. 82, quotes Averroes as saying of him:

'One day you are a Yemenite when you meet a man from Yemen,
But when you see someone from Ma'add you assert you are from 'Adnān!'

7. Thus he has firmly adopted the doctrine from philosophy and philosophical mysticism that man is the soul and not soul-and-body; the body has been given to man partly as an evil to contend against (as a test) and partly as an initial instrument. This doctrine which appears in both types of treatises, is, coupled, emphatically in exoteric treatises, with the resurrection, or rather re-creation of the body. In the esoteric treatises (e.g. *Ma'ārij al-Quds*, Cairo, 1927, p. 167, and *al-Maḍnūn al-Kabīr*, Cairo, 1309 A.H., p. 22) the resurrection of the body is weakly and evasively treated and is accompanied by an account of life after death, which is taken *en bloc* from Avicenna. I find Ibn Taymīya's description (op. cit., p. 79) of him (offered, of course, as a condemnation) very apt, 'His statements are mid-way between the Muslims' and the philosophers'; in him you find a mixture of philosophy and Islam'.

8. Both in the preface and at the end of this work (pp. 4 and 210), al-Ghazālī uses the expression 'to be guarded against those who are not fit for it (al-maḍnūn bihā 'alā ghayr-i-ahlihā)' which is also the title of another esoteric treatise.

9. This is the line of thought followed also in his *Munqidh* which he wrote at 'about the age of fifty' (preface): 'Beyond reason there is another grade in which another eye is opened by which one sees the Unseen and the future and other things as inaccessible to reason as intelligibles are to the discriminative (cogitative) faculty . . . etc.' (Section on Prophecy). Like Ibn Ḥazm, al-Ghazālī also says here that sciences like medicine and astronomy are a result of prophetic revelation. So far as the essential nature of prophecy goes, there seems little difference between the *Ma'ārij* and the *Munqidh*.

10. It is this idea with which al-Ghazālī, in his *Tahāfut*, opposes Avicenna's conception of imaginative prophecy as an almost automatic and autonomous contact of the prophet's mind with the souls of the heavenly bodies which contain all knowledge of the future in themselves as a matter of natural phenomenon and not as being under the direction of God.

11. In this work we find both philosophy and official Islam expressed philosophically, but virtually no mysticism as such. May it have been written before 488 A.H., the year when as the author says in the *Munqidh*, he adopted mysticism?

12. There is again little evidence as to the date of this work. Although the author says (p. 74) 'This (Islamic) Sharī'a is five hundred years old', this is most probably not meant in a precise sense. I regard it, however, very likely that the work was written late in the author's life and later than *Ma'ārij al-Quds*.

13. Al-Shahrastānī, *Nihāyat al-Iqdām fī 'ilm al-Kalām*, ed. A. Guillaume, p. 426, 6 sq.

14. ibid, p. 463, 1–4.

15. ibid, p. 462, 12–14.

16. ibid, pp. 425, 18–26, 3.

17. ibid, 429, 6 sq.

18. I have left out in this notice the long discussions about miracles and their evidentiary status, although they form by far the greater part of the Kalām-teaching on prophecy.

19. *Muqaddima*, Bulaq, p. 81, 8–9.

20. ibid, p. 81, 17–23.

21. This three-fold classification is on p. 82, 16 sq.

22. ibid, p. 83, 7 sq.

23. Averroes, *De Anima* (Camb., Mass., 1953, pp. 406, 30–407, 5): Quoniam opinati sumus ex hoc sermone quod intellectus materialis est unicus omnibus hominibus, et etiam ex hoc sumus opinati quod species humana est aeterna . . . etc. (According to Averroes, the active and the potential intellects are not two substances but one.)

INDEX